P9-APE-099

SMART START

SMART START

ELEMENTARY EDUCATION FOR THE 21ST CENTURY

Patte Barth
Ruth Mitchell

Sponsored by The Council for Basic Education

NORTH AMERICAN PRESS

Golden, Colorado

Book and cover design by Peggy Robertson Design
Photography by John Booz
Cover photograph by Gale Zucker

Library of Congress Cataloging-in-Publication Data

Barth, Patte

Smart start : elementary education for the 21st century / Patte Barth, Ruth Mitchell ; photographs by John Booz ; cover photograph by Gale Zucker ; sponsored by the Council for Basic Education. Washington, D.C.

p. cm.

Includes bibliographical references (p.) and index.

ISBN 1-55591-908-1

1. Education, Elementary—United States. 2. Educational change—United States. 3. Education, Elementary—United States—Evaluation.I. Mitchell, Ruth, 1933- . II. Council for Basic Education. III. Title.

LA219.B37 1992 92-60659
372.973—dc20 CIP

Printed in the United States of America

0 9 8 7 6 5 4 3 2 1

North American Press
350 Indiana Street
Golden, Colorado 80401-5093
USA

CONTENTS

ACKNOWLEDGMENTS

SMART START was developed with the support of the John D. and Catherine T. MacArthur Foundation. We acknowledge the early drafts written by Dennis Gray and Rona Wilensky. We also thank the Board of Directors for the Council for Basic Education (CBE) for their patience in reading two drafts of this book, and we are particularly grateful to the following for their advice and comments: A. Graham Down, President of the Council for Basic Education; Mrs. Talcott Bates; Mrs. Barry Bingham, Sr.; Charles Blitzer; Charlotte Brooks; Rexford Brown; Carl Dolce; Kermeen Fristrom; Melinda Martin; Thomas Payzant; Dr. Diane Ravitch; and Mrs. Keith Wellin. Above all, we thank Peter Gerber, education program officer of the MacArthur Foundation, for his generous help and support and gratefully offer him the fruits of his patience.

We dedicate this vision to elementary teachers in the nation's schools who understand how far their every action and word may carry in their students' lives, for better or for worse.

INTRODUCTION

A DISASTER IN THE MAKING

IN SPRING OF 1993, a national examination will probably be available at grade 4 in reading, writing, and mathematics. Although participation in the examination will be voluntary for states and districts, many will choose to take part because the examination will tell educators and the public where their students stand in regard to a national standard.

The results of the grade 4 examination in 1993 will be abysmal. We know already from the results of the National Assessment of Educational Progress that children can perform acceptably at low levels of skill but cannot perform well when thinking and problem solving are required. In the national examinations, both thinking and problem solving will be required. At grade 4, children will be expected to read literature and relate its meaning to their own lives; they will be expected to solve quantitative problems and explain why their solution worked.

They can't do these things now, at grade 4 or any other grade. They can't because they haven't been taught. Their teachers were trained to dish out information in tiny chunks and rush on to the next chunk. The teachers were not asked to connect the chunks to make meaning or help the students to do so.

The dismal results we can expect in 1993 (and those we have already seen on traditional tests such as the state-by-state National Assessment of Education Progress reported in June 1991) are the consequence of teaching directed toward wrong ends in the wrong way.

Meaning at the center

The voluntary national examination will be unlike anything known in this country before. It will be taken by all students at grade 4 — not a sample, as in the case of the present National Assessment of Educational Progress. And it will be based on curricular frameworks arrived at through consensus among professionals about the quality of what children should know and be able to do in literacy and mathematics.

In form, the examination may be partly the familiar multiple-choice questions, but most of it will consist of the three p's: *performances*, such as writing samples and reading aloud; *portfolios* of writing and mathematics selected to display a wide range of abilities as they grow over time; and *projects*, either individual or group, that will demonstrate children's problem solving and communicative skills.

Because there isn't enough time between now and spring 1993 for teachers to regear their teaching completely, the function of the voluntary national examination will be to point a direction for elementary education. It will model a kind of instruction that can be found only in a minority of elementary schools now. The form and content of the examination is specifically intended to drive instruction. Schooling is centered on the active construction of meaning by students. That is, reading, writing, and mathematics are activities intended to make the world and ourselves understandable.

This book envisions a curriculum and pedagogy for an elementary school where the children would be thoroughly prepared for the grade 4 national examination. So prepared, in fact, that they probably wouldn't notice that it was taking place, because some of its components — performances, portfolios, and projects —

are normal practice. What we describe here is in line with the multifaceted national examination, not because we are writing a primer for it, but because our curriculum is based on the same frameworks and curricula as those guiding the framers of the national examination. Elementary education has changed direction, away from basal readers, rote learning, and worksheets, and toward literature, thinking, problem solving, and writing in all areas.

Our curriculum focus

Consistent with the principles of the CBE, this report on elementary education is concerned with the academic content of schooling. The word "basic" in the name of the Council for Basic Education means the academic bedrock that education must provide each and every citizen: **literacy**, meaning communicative ability in all forms and in all subjects across the curriculum; **mathematics**, especially problem solving; **science** as a means of understanding ourselves and our world; **history** as an exciting narrative of change and development; the **arts**, both as object of study and of production; and at least one **language** in addition to English.

By elementary education, we mean the years between kindergarten and grade 6. For our purposes elementary education goes to about age twelve. We recognize that in our decentralized system elementary education can end at any grade between 5 and 8, but we chose a cutoff point that is still the most common and which marks the natural division between childhood and adolescence for most children.

Because of our emphasis on academic achievement, this report complements other current work that focuses on the social and physical development of young children. We understand the importance of the social and physical context of elementary education. We have read the reports about the poverty, disease, neglect, and hopelessness pervading the inner cities, and indeed, we devote a good deal of discussion to these issues; but we insist that the business of the classroom is students' academic learning.

We think of elementary school as the first steps in the education of citizens who realize their full potential—they work productively, vote and understand what they are voting for, and enjoy learning throughout their lives. They are able to participate in their society fully and criticize it constructively. We emphasize that this curriculum is for *all* students. The school has the duty and responsibility to enable all children to learn, no matter what background they come from or what their preparation is.

Our first section acknowledges that this is a tall order, as we look at the background of many elementary school students in the 1990s and present ways of dealing with the consequences in the schools. Section Two expounds four important principles upon which our curriculum is based and explains why they are fundamental.

In Section Three the contents of the curriculum are spelled out. These are based on published statements by professional associations such as the National Council of Teachers of Mathematics, the National Council of Teachers of English, and the National Council for the Social Studies, as well as summarized frameworks for the National Assessment of Educational Progress, and state frameworks and guidelines, especially those issued by the California Department of Education.

A consensus on meaningful education is clear from these documents. Despite the difference in academic subject matter, they all agree that education must center on important concepts, not mere facts; it must foster active learning, not passive memorization; it must help children become responsible for their own progress; and it must connect the classroom to the real world. These factors have been derived from published frameworks and guidelines that are also the basis for national standards.

Section Four lists eight conditions necessary for all students in all elementary schools to master the curriculum. In Section Five we take the reader into a classroom where the principles are honored and a good deal of our recommended curriculum is in place. We provide running commentary so that the reader can understand how the classroom activities translate the principles and the curriculum.

The final section lists recommendations for the adults who can make a difference – perhaps not in time for the first national examination in spring 1993 but within a few years – such as administrators, parents, teachers and those who prepare them, and legislators.

SMART START

SECTION ONE

WHAT'S WRONG

CHILDREN PRESENTLY in the fifth grade and under will graduate from high school in the twenty-first century. They will almost certainly live to see Comet Halley swing by the earth in 2061. But the conditions in which they will live and the condition of the earth itself are the responsibility of our school system here and now.

We can't brush off concern by saying that we won't be around then, so why should we worry?[1] At the basest level of self interest, we, especially the parents of the elementary school children who will live the bulk of their lives in the twenty-first century, must be concerned about an economy to provide support and medical care in their old age. In 1960 the economy absorbed so many

Fundamental Responsibility

From the first day of kindergarten, most children are taught that they should not set their own goals for learning or construct their own learning programs. Schools, they are taught, will do this for them. Schools thus abdicate a fundamental responsibility: that of showing children how to improve the learning strategies they have already constructed for themselves. Children will learn spontaneously. What they need help in, from experts, is how to learn better.[2]

workers that each person on Social Security was supported by the contributions of seventeen workers; in 1992 a retiree will be supported by only three workers.[3]

Our present decisions and actions to educate elementary children must rest on a coherent vision of development toward responsible, flexible, intelligent governance of a planet with finite resources and dreadful fragility.

Concern for our personal futures is a legitimate reason to urge the education of productive workers, but it lacks vision. In a nation that first modeled democracy to the world, there are surely more inspiring reasons to urge immediate attention to the quality of elementary education. For the first time in history, the future of the planet itself is in our power. It is not possible to make a division between the future and the present—decisions made now reflect our hopes for the future. So our present decisions and actions to educate elementary children must rest on a coherent vision of development toward responsible, flexible, intelligent governance of a planet with finite resources and dreadful fragility. What happens in the classroom now is affected by whether we think we are educating space-colonizing pioneers, participants in "global webs" producing world-shrinking technology,[4] machine-tenders, or manual laborers.

Wanted: A vision

The basic problem is that American education doesn't know what it wants to produce. "School" is a ritual for a large number—perhaps the majority—of Americans. It seems unconnected with their lives outside school or with their futures, and it is largely a place for socializing. We are constantly reminded by reports on education and the economy that a good record in school, especially high school, is important only to the small minority competing for places in prestigious and selective colleges. For the rest, a high school diploma is granted for attendance and seat time, both sometimes minimal, and, because we have no apprenticeship system, the diploma lacks consequences for students going into the work force.[5]

American education used to know what it wanted to produce and did it quite well: It produced a leadership elite in expensive private schools (mostly in New England and on the east coast); a managerial class that attended state universities and colleges; and a large corps of workers who could read, write, and compute enough to work on the assembly lines that made America rich and its population prosperous in the middle years of this century.

The problem is that public education is designed to keep on producing the managers and the workers, although the world doesn't want them any longer. The educational production line is geared only to produce bolt-tighteners on assembly lines, when the rest of the world uses robots operated by technicians who read computer screens to command the robots.

The American public education system has to redesign and retool completely for a world where ability to respond to messages on a computer screen is a more valuable asset than ability to follow orders.

New schools for new challenges

The American public education system has to redesign and retool completely for a world where ability to respond to messages on a computer screen is a more valuable asset than ability to follow orders. Redesigning the system is hampered by its decentralized bureaucracy: It's like a grotesquely oversized animal that can't move more quickly than one mile an hour because the messages take minutes to get from brain to leg muscles. Our competitors in the industrialized world (and many in the Third World) have central control over education and in most cases a cultural tradition of respect for educational authority. The U.S. federal government has a minimal role in education; research, data-gathering, and ensuring compliance with regulations are the main functions of the U.S. Department of Education. The fifty states, the District of Columbia, and the territories all have their own education policies and their own state education departments. Then the sixteen thousand school boards in the country make policy that is carried out in the classroom.

The National Governors' Association's 1991 report, *From Rhetoric to Action*,[6] tries to put a good face on what is essentially a patchwork. Some states are just piloting what in other states is established policy; one or two have completely rethought their education system, while a couple of others may repeal their education improvement legislation. The incoherence causes the beast to stumble along at a snail's pace, although the system needs the gazelle's ability to change direction instantly.

If radical change were introduced from kindergarten upward, teachers and students would not need to "unlearn" inappropriate habits at higher grades when they have become engrained. Changing the schools year by year would also give reformers time to negotiate with the higher education institutions whose demands now drive the high school curriculum and frequently thwart improvements. Such a logical approach is too much to hope.

A coherent plan to retool American schools for the lifetime of the youngest in them would begin with kindergarten and the elementary school, and then implement the changes as the children grow.

An insidious myth also influences reformers and turns their attentions from elementary schools toward middle schools and high schools—the myth that elementary schools are doing a good job, under the circumstances. William Bennett says in *First Lessons* that "American elementary education is not menaced by a rising 'tide of mediocrity.' It is, overall, in pretty good shape."[7] Others have called elementary education "the jewel in the crown" of American education.

Looking at the miserable products of American education, with a nearly 25 percent dropout rate nationwide (75 percent in some inner city schools), semi-illiterate graduates who can't perform simple tasks, college students whose skills are so far below expectation that universities have to establish special departments to remediate them, and widespread ignorance of basic history, geography, and science, these complacent estimates seem odd. How can the top end be so unsatisfactory if the foundation is solid? The results belie confidence in the elementary school. If it were doing a pretty good job, then we could expect better performance at the higher levels.

We have to confront another myth about elementary education: Elementary schools would do a good job if the children arrived ready to learn. *We contend that schools must be designed so that children will learn no matter what they bring or do not bring from their family background.* This is a fighting statement. Its implications must be understood and acted on if American education is to serve its constituents properly.

The myth of unreadiness

A myth is by definition a story told to explain phenomena. The story in this case is that schools cannot teach children who come to school hungry, without adequate parental care, undisciplined, even drug-addicted from birth.[8] Please note that the myth concerns the schools' response to these conditions: There is no possible dispute about how bad the conditions are.

We have to confront another myth about elementary education: Elementary schools would do a good job if the children arrived ready to learn. We contend that schools must be designed so that children will learn no matter what they bring or do not bring from their family background.

The kindergarten class that entered school in September 1991 (and the students born in 1986) consisted of a majority of what we used to call "minority" children in four states, California, Texas, New Mexico, and Mississippi, and in most large urban districts.[9] Because poverty afflicts African Americans, Native Americans, Hispanic Americans, and immigrants more than other sectors of the population, a large number of 1991's kindergartners are poor.[10] In the age group of their parents, who are primarily in their twenties, three-quarters of families headed by single women, even with a high school diploma, are poor. For families headed by female high school dropouts, the poverty rate is almost 90 percent.[11] The children from these families may be ill-nourished or have medical problems that have not been treated for lack of money to pay medical bills. Some of them were born with a drug addiction because their mothers used cocaine or heroin.[12]

Of one hundred of these kindergartners selected randomly, only forty-one will grow up in the traditional family setting of two parents and siblings. Twelve of the one hundred will be born to unmarried mothers, many of them teenagers; the parents of forty-five of these children will either divorce or separate before the child reaches eighteen; and two of the one hundred will see a parent die in their childhood.[13]

Despite their differences, most of these kindergartners have one thing in common: They have watched a lot of television. Nielsen estimates that the television set is on for six hours and fifty-five minutes a day in the average American household, and nearly seventy hours a week in African-American households.[14] The 1992

kindergartners are the grandchildren of the first television generation. Their parents, now about twenty-five or thirty years old, grew up in the television age, and have no memory of a time when radio and newspapers largely played the role now filled by television. Television is the background to these parents' lives, so they cannot be expected to see it as a rival to reading for pleasure. We should also remember that not only the parents of our kindergartners but also their teachers are to some extent television babies. Nothing definite seems to be known about the effects of television on teaching and learning, although there is some evidence that watching television — even shows like *Sesame Street* — reinforces shortness of attention span.[15] Research into the effects of television on cognition is needed to guide pedagogy suited to a generation of children who have largely learned how the world works from the screen.

In some parts of the country the kindergartners will speak another language.[16] The largest number of these children speak Spanish, but some, especially on the west coast, will speak Korean, Chinese, and Southeast Asian languages. The teacher's challenge in many cases will be confronting a group of children who speak several different languages with only a few speaking English. School thus begins for some children without a common language with their classmates or the teacher.

The tyranny of the norm

What does the school system do with them? It treats them all the same.

An immense variety of children comes into the schools as kindergartners every year. Quite apart from the expected individual differences among human beings, these children speak different dialects or different languages, belong to cultures with their origins across the globe, are different in physical heritage and skin color, and vary enormously in their understanding of what school is all about.

What does the school system do with them? It treats them all the same.

The norm governs the school's dealings with children. Even during the kindergarten year, there may be norm-referenced tests of readiness for academic work. In first grade, children are grouped for reading and mathematics according to their perceived proximity to the norm – a standard derived from the so-called normal distribution along a bell curve. Textbooks are written, materials devised, and teachers trained to deal with children who conform. Expectations for intellectual growth throughout the year are geared to the fairly small number of children in the center of the normal distribution.

The children are expected to learn to read in the same way from the same basal reader. They are expected to be able to memorize the multiplication tables and other arithmetical facts at the same rate as the norm dictates. They are expected to know what behavior is expected in school and to understand that "teacher talk" is a special kind of discourse requiring a special "school" response from them. And, as Sylvia Farnham-Diggory says in the epigraph to this chapter, they are expected to yield to the school control over their learning processes. You must learn our way, not yours, is the message that comes across loud and clear to young children.

The results of treating all children as if they learned in the same way at the same rate should be obvious, even predictable, to educators. America's children aren't learning very well or very much. At age nine (grade 4), only about 15 percent of American students can read well enough to search for specific information, relate ideas to each other, and summarize the general meaning of a passage. Fewer than 20 percent of age nine students can solve a mathematics problem such as this: "There are ten airplanes on the ground. Six take off and four more land. How many are still on the ground?" It is positively frightening that only 5 percent – one in twenty – African-American students can handle such problems at age nine.[17]

The results of treating all children as if they learned in the same way at the same rate should be obvious, even predictable, to educators. America's children aren't learning very well or very much.

The school assembly line

The teachers are caught in a trap they didn't design but can't recognize or escape. Here is a typical example: A frustrated fourth-grade teacher waves a stack of test papers at a visitor and complains, "Look at these math tests. Half of them are F's. Well, it's too late to do anything about it now. Next week we move on to long division."

The fourth-grade children trying to learn math in such a classroom are like Charlie Chaplin in *Modern Times* frantically trying to keep pace with the ever-increasing speed of the factory assembly line. Turn the screw on the widget, recite the multiplication tables; can't worry about the one missed because the shop steward is rapidly sending through more widgets, more lessons. The image would be comic if the minds of children were not at stake. It is important to note that these children are no more incapable of learning math than Charlie Chaplin is of turning out a pretty good widget. The problem in both cases is that the decisions governing production are made on the basis of "normal" expectation of progress and implemented without regard to actual performance. Charlie Chaplin's character went crazy, ran from the assembly line, and began using his two spanners on anything the same distance apart as the bolts he was trained to tighten. The teacher moves up the assembly line of math lessons to long division, even though the children have not yet mastered earlier material.

Evading the issue—tracking

When children cannot meet the expectations of a norm-bound curriculum, the school responds by putting them into low, remedial tracks or even into special education classes.

Children who come from economically impoverished, chaotic, and even violent homes are unlikely to perform according to the school norm. These children, as we mentioned above, are predominantly African American, Native American, Hispanic American, and immigrant. The inflexibility of the schools combines with the students' inadequate preparation for formal instruction to produce a frequently disastrous outcome. By third or fourth grade, these children have academically fallen behind their peers from white, middle-class homes. By middle school, the average minority child is more than a year behind on standardized, norm-referenced tests. When they leave school, average minority students will achieve at about the level of white middle-class thirteen-year-olds, as judged by results on the National Assessment of Educational Progress.[18]

When children cannot meet the expectations of a norm-bound curriculum, the school responds by putting them into low, remedial tracks or even into special education classes. In 1989, special education classes in Boston public schools were 25 percent minority,[19] a far larger proportion than their share of the population.

Once assigned to a slow track, to special education, or to a repeated grade, these children are programmed for failure. Many of them will probably drop out of school since retention in grade and assignment outside the "normal" stream are strong indicators of later dropout.[20] They are like Jorge, an eight-year-old who has already begun dropping out of school. "Too often," his teacher says, "he reverses written figures" (a "normal" eight-year-old does not reverse written figures). He hesitates when reading out loud. The teacher wants him classified "learning disabled" and placed in the special education class.

Once identified as not conforming to expectations for their age, children are compartmentalized accordingly, whether in discreet, special classes, as in Jorge's case, or grouped within the classroom by their perceived ability with such things as reading and numbers. So pervasive now is the concept of ability groupings that even liberally minded teachers and parents see it as an effective and mutually reinforcing method of encouraging all children to learn, contending that it enables children to learn at their own rates.

Children identified as gifted gain wherever they are placed, but the needy lose from isolation in ability groups.

It is true that children learn differently and at different rates. But it is also true that the early — *and often faulty* — identification of children as slow or fast learners remains with them throughout their school careers, regardless of any emotional or cognitive "catching up" that may actually occur. Current research, notably that of Robert Slavin at Johns Hopkins University, further indicts ability grouping by showing that while there are virtually no benefits to those classified as fast learners that would not also be available in integrated groupings, there is considerable evidence to indicate that the other children, the "slower" children, suffer.[21] The gifted gain wherever they are placed, but the needy lose from isolation in ability groups. These children, far from being brought up to the higher level but at a different rate, are more often stuck in a curricular routine of mundane seat work, lower expectations, and content-thin lessons. Moreover, once categorized, children rarely move from one group to the other, whatever their actual abilities. The result: The "slower" children get an inferior education.

They know it, and a number of them don't stick around for the complete dose.

The way to Hell

Although our language may occasionally convey otherwise without our intention, we must make it clear that there is no malice in the school system. No one is doing a poor job on purpose. We are talking about turning round the beast whose brain doesn't send messages clearly or quickly to a myriad of legs. The messages say that the times have changed, the school population has changed, and the understanding of cognitive acquisition has changed.

Most of the teachers in U.S. elementary schools do not have degrees in an academic subject.[22] They have degrees in education, so methods courses displaced academic subjects from their program. Furthermore, these methods courses were based on an outmoded understanding of human cognition.[23] Teachers were educated to think of knowledge as a ladder students climb with skills. Skills must precede knowledge. Anything taught can be cut up into little bits so that it can be absorbed easily. Children must prove that they know each little bit before they can move on to the next one. If they can't prove it (usually by taking a multiple-choice, norm-referenced test or the teacher's version of one), they must repeat the step by filling out worksheets. From this view of cognition as a ladder—with only a vague sense of where the ladder reaches—naturally flow basal readers, tracking, worksheets, and the detachment from the real world that children sense immediately in school.

Instead, cognitive science has established that "human minds are constructed to deal with richly complex environments, to make sense out of their experiences, and to store knowledge that is useful in coping with new ones."[24] Understanding learning as the absorption of new information into existing schemata, the making of connections with former learning, entails a different pedagogy, one that centralizes meaning. But the message that cognition is an active search to understand the world hasn't got to all the limbs of the elementary education beast yet. Test publishers still believe there are skills that must be learned and tested before children can approach knowledge,[25] and teachers for the most part still operate on that principle. Worse, parents expect skill-ladder teaching, because they were taught that way themselves and can see no reason why their children shouldn't go through the same process.[26]

Everyone has good intentions, but they don't all have good information.

Sending an urgent message

There is one way to make sure that something gets taught – test it. The truth of this has become more and more apparent since the beginning of the 1980s, when, as a result of clarion calls like *Nation at Risk*, legislatures urged accountability on the schools. The means of accountability were multiple-choice norm-referenced tests, and before long administrators were monitoring what teachers taught to make sure it was aligned with the tests. Teachers began to teach in that form: They would write a question on the board and then list a, b, and c alternatives for an answer.

There is one way to make sure that something gets taught—test it.

Multiple-choice, norm-referenced testing corrupts teaching because it is essentially passive – students select, they do not construct, an answer. It gives the false impression that answers are "right" or "wrong"; it asks for memorization or retention of algorithms, not understanding; it does not provide accurate information about what children know and can do, because they aren't asked to demonstrate knowledge or skill; it trivializes schooling—all the effort for a few bubbles on a scantron sheet; and it focuses on what can easily be tested, not what is important.[27] In this list can be recognized some of the same criticisms that we have made of teaching—and it is not a coincidence.

If we get multiple-choice teaching when we test by multiple choice, why wouldn't we get hands-on, conceptual teaching if we test that way?

But the causal relationship between testing and teaching has positive as well as negative aspects. If we get multiple-choice teaching when we test by multiple choice, why wouldn't we get hands-on, conceptual teaching if we test that way? Douglas Reynolds, science supervisor in the New York State Education Department, reasoned thus when he instituted the grade 4 Manipulative Skills Test of the Elementary Science Program Evaluation Test in May 1989. Despairing of getting hands-on science into grades K through 4, Reynolds arranged for each grade 4 in New York to take a test consisting of five "stations" where students had to weigh, measure, predict, classify, and observe using the appropriate physical apparatus—a balance, a ruler, a thermometer, a closed box with something rattling in it, an electrical circuit, and so on. He was sending a message through the test: Early elementary students should have these experiences in science classes. It worked. At the least, New York students are now taught to use the five pieces of apparatus, and some get much more experience if they have teachers with an interest in and knowledge of science.

The California Department of Education used the "what you test is what gets taught" principle in designing their statewide writing assessment, so that students in grades 8 and 12 now learn to write eight genres of writing and their appropriate rhetorical techniques. Open-ended mathematics questions on the California Assessment Program's grade 12 test are now reinforcing problem solving and communication in mathematics, as students write explanations of their solutions.

The technique is spreading as states and districts become aware that schools must change and that assessment is a potent tool to budge them. The reading assessment for the National Assessment of Education Progress at grade 4 in 1992 asks students for responses to three kinds of reading: for pleasure, for information, and for instructions to perform a task.[28]

As we said in the introduction, the voluntary national examination in spring 1993 will use methods of assessment that teachers should be using for instruction in the classroom. The message could hardly be sent more clearly or more urgently.

Elementary principles

How can elementary schools be held to account for the performance of children who arrive in school with the social and economic disadvantages listed earlier? Is it fair to expect the schools to overcome the influence of poor health, poor nutrition, years of passively watching television, violence in the home and on the street, and indifference from adults?

It is fair to expect schools to do their business, that is, to attend to the academic needs of children. Schools cannot be social welfare agencies, although they should work in close cooperation with them. We believe that elementary schools should share buildings or at least be neighbors with health and counseling clinics. Academic achievement *is* the school's business. Teaching means bridging the gap between the learner and what is to be learned. Teachers should see themselves not as technicians with textbooks, but as possessors of special skills and as translators of knowledge into terms children – all sorts of children – can understand.

Teaching means bridging the gap between the learner and what is to be learned. Teachers should see themselves not as technicians with textbooks, but as possessors of special skills and as translators of knowledge into terms children—all sorts of children—can understand.

The first principle of the elementary school should be that children are individuals and learn at their own rates and in their own way – and they all want to learn.[29] The teacher should adapt to the children's own speed and style of learning, using every possible technique, method, and trick to communicate with them. The teacher must expect the same ability to learn in each child, no matter how hostile, withdrawn, or indifferent. Children are not "dumb" because they behave in ways not acceptable to the school norm.

Shirley Brice Heath sheds light on cultural differences in the backgrounds of children in "What No Bedtime Story Means: Narrative Skills at Home and School," a description of three kinds of home backgrounds.[30] In Maintown, a middle-class white suburb, the child is read to each evening and is asked questions of the same sort that teachers ask in school: "What's that? Who's that? What does the doggie say?" A second child from a white working-class home, Roadville, is taught the alphabet by caretakers but is not encouraged to tell stories that may be regarded as "lies" by the strictly religious community. The third child is African American, from Trackton, where he is almost constantly in physical contact with other people and feels secure and loved. But the adults do not read to him and believe that it wouldn't do any good anyway. Children "come to know," they say.

The first principle of the elementary school should be that children are individuals and learn at their own rates and in their own way—and they all want to learn. Children are not "dumb" because they behave in ways not acceptable to the school norm.

These three children will end up in the same class at school. Obviously, in the prevailing educational mode, the middle-class white child will have no trouble with school, the white working-class child will do well at the early stages and then cease to understand what is wanted, and the African-American child will simply not comprehend from the beginning. If the teacher has not read Heath's anthropological studies, or does not have the same expectations for all three children, the outcome will mirror what the children brought as input.

But if the teacher takes the differences between these children as the central challenge of the job, he will realize that all of them need special treatment. The African-American child needs to be treated as James Comer treats poor African-American children in New Haven, Connecticut, schools:[31] The teacher works with the child's parents to explain the purposes of school to them and ask their cooperation in encouraging the child to read. The white working-class child need stimuli to extend the range of her reading. The middle-class child is not without needs, despite the advantage of early socialization which prepares the child for school. As Heath says, "Mainstream children can benefit from early exposure to Trackton's creative, highly analogical styles of telling stories and giving explanations, and they can add the Roadville true story with strict chronicity and explicit moral to their repertoire of narrative types."[32]

All three, like all the other children in the class and in the school, must be held to the same high standard – but what is expected must be made clear to them and to their parents. The lists of expected academic achievement in Section Three are examples of the kind of information that should be available to everyone concerned, including the students themselves. If these standards are not met, the school – the administration and the teachers – should be held responsible, not the students.

Although it is fair to expect that all students should achieve at the same high standard with the school's help, it is not fair to expect this result with present resources. Education is the stepchild of American society. It is inadequately funded because it is infrastructure to our bottom-line economy and produces no wealth directly. Short-sighted legislators do not perceive it as they should: the nation's most important investment for the future.

The major resource is the teachers' professional skill. Now woefully lacking in too many cases, the professional development of teachers is our most pressing need. Teachers can't be expected to change their teaching techniques without enlarging their repertoire, trying out new ideas, refining them and being allowed time for all this. We propose that teachers should be year-round employees like other professionals, but should spend at least two months of the year in academic study and professional renewal.

Other resources are available at less expense. Americans are growing older and remaining healthier at the same time, so a pool of retired talent will soon develop. Older people should be asked to spend part of a day in a school, perhaps paid, perhaps as volunteers, to listen to a child read, help with a project, even simply to converse with children who have not had much experience talking to adults.

The major resource is the teachers' professional skill.

Besides the cost of professional skill and assistance, the schools' other crying need is for technology. It should be a matter of shame to American society that schools still use purple-ink ditto machines to reproduce teaching material, while the rest of the world uses photcopying machines – some of which sort, staple, and practically read the material for you. Some teachers use computers effectively, but too many, especially teachers of the humanities, are computer-shy and have no professional opportunity to overcome their reluctance. Children now in school will work in a technology-rich culture, but schools are not yet preparing them for it. Texas has adopted videodiscs as well as textbooks, although we are skeptical about the number of teachers who will use them to their fullest potential – or use them at all. All mathematics curriculum frameworks tell teachers that children should use calculators from their earliest days in school and scientific calculators as soon as they can understand them. However, outmoded fears that arithmetical skills will trophy if calculators perform computations combine with lack of money to keep calculator use from becoming universal.

Children now in school will work in a technology-rich culture, but schools are not yet preparing them for it.

Not letting schools off the hook

School reform proceeds in waves. Early in the 1980s, schools raised the number of credits needed to graduate and universities tightened entrance requirements. A year or two later, teacher education and career ladders were the answer. Then curriculum frameworks. Mostly recently, restructuring. Now every report urges getting parents involved in their children's education. The Committee for Economic Development puts parent involvement on an equal footing with school improvement: "First, the nation must redefine education as a process that begins at birth, recognizing that the potential for learning begins even earlier. Second, the schools must be better prepared to help children become educated. . . ."[33] We don't think it wise to put so much emphasis on parental involvement because in case of failure, the schools have an excuse. "We can't do the second because parents didn't do the first" may be heard in response to the Committee for Economic Development.

Schools must take the children as they arrive and adapt their techniques—but not their standards—to their needs.

We feel uneasy about the National Education Association's emphasis on prenatal care for the same reasons.

Schools must take the children as they arrive and adapt their techniques – but not their standards – to their needs. Yes, they need additional resources, but even lack of resources should not let the schools off the hook. They are society's guardians of essential knowledge and should regard their duty as a sacred trust.

NOTES

1. For a discussion of attitudes on the future, see Robert Heilbroner, *An Inquiry into the Human Prospect*, especially 169–176.
2. Sylvia Farnham-Diggory, *Schooling*, 49.
3. Harold Hodgkinson, *All One System*, 3.
4. Robert Reich, *The Work of Nations*, passim.
5. As a result of "Where We Stand" columns by Al Shanker of the American Federation of Teachers in the *New York Times* (the first on this subject was dated 16 July 1989) and Shanker's frequent public speeches, this has almost become a truism. An eloquent statement of the problem and a practical solution for it can be found in the report of the Commission on the Skills of the American Workforce, National Center on Education and the Economy, *America's Choice: High Skills or Low Wages,* and in an article by John Bishop, "Why the Apathy in American High Schools?" *Educational Researcher*, 18:1 (January/February 1989): 6–10.
6. National Governors' Association, *From Rhetoric to Action,* 1991.
7. William Bennett, *First Lessons*, 1.
8. Harold Hodgkinson, "Reform Versus Reality," 8–16.
9. Quality Education for Minorities Project, *Education that Works*, 11.
10. Committee for Economic Development, *The Unfinished Agenda*, 8.

11. However, 20 percent of the population defined as "the underclass" because of poverty and social problems is white, according to recent research by the Urban Institute. Looking primarily at large metropolitan areas conceals the size of the white underclass, which is located in small neighborhoods in medium-sized cities, says the researcher, Ronald B. Mincy, *The Urban Institute Policy and Research Report*, 24.
12. In 1989, 11 percent of all babies born were exposed to illegal drugs, according to the National Commission to Prevent Infant Mortality. These children will enter kindergarten in 1995.
13. Harold Hodgkinson, *All One System,* 3.
14. Based on data from November 1990. Nielsen Media Research, New York.
15. "Why Sesame Street is Bad News for Reading," *Education Week* (19 September 1990): 32.
16. In twenty-eight states, more than 1 percent of the children in school are Limited English Proficient (LEP). The state with the highest proportion of LEP students is New Mexico, where one in five children is designated LEP; California has 14 percent LEP; and Alaska has 10 percent. (National Clearinghouse for Bilingual Education, 1990.)
17. Educational Testing Service Policy Information Center, *Performance at the Top*, 4, 6.
18. Quality Education for Minorities Project, *Education That Works*, 18.
19. Massachusetts Advocacy Center, *Locked In/Locked Out,* 24.
20. Lorrie A. Shepard and Mary Lee Smith, "Synthesis of Research on Grade Retention," 84–88.
21. Robert E. Slavin, "Synthesis of Research on Tracking," 67–76.
22. Only California requires teachers to have a degree in an academic subject before they may train as teachers, although a few others specify concentrations in the liberal arts for teacher candidates. (*Manual on Certification and Preparation of Edu-*

cational Personnel in the U.S., National Association of State Directors of Teacher Education and Certification, 1988.) Recent reforms have increased the number of states where academic undergraduate degrees will be required, but these reforms will not affect the pool of teachers for at least four years.

23. A brief but trenchant criticism of elementary teacher training can be found in Martin Haberman's article, "Thirty-One Reasons to Stop the School Reading Machine," especially reasons 21 through 24. Haberman is a professor of education at the University of Wisconsin, Milwaukee, and a credible critic of teacher education.
24. Sylvia Farnham-Diggory, *Schooling*, 56.
25. A test publisher used these words in a February 1990 ABC News Special on new forms of educational assessment in defense of his company's products.
26. Gerald Bracey, "Advocates of Basic Skills," 32.
27. Summarized from Chapter One of Ruth Mitchell, *Testing for Learning.*
28. When some teachers read the National Assessment Governing Board's *Looking at How Well Our Students Read*, the framework of expectations for the 1992 national reading test, they found it difficult to understand that there would be no vocabulary or comprehension questions.
29. Haberman in "Thirty-One Reasons to Stop the School Reading Machine" says that children have been observed in university education department laboratory schools to begin reading at any age from three through eleven, and "How old they were when they learned had little or no effect on their ultimate progress through school and in life" (284).
30. Shirley Brice Heath, "What No Bedtime Story Means," 49–76.
31. Comer, "Educating Poor Minority Children," 42–48.

32. Ibid.
33. Committee for Economic Development, *The Unfinished Agenda,* 5.

SECTION TWO

A STATEMENT OF PRINCIPLES

IT IS NO longer feasible, either practically or morally, to lose one-quarter of our students and to advance the rest with mixed results. Obviously, the lock-step factory model and the practice of tracking young children into different ability groups must go. The model and its parts should be replaced by a vision of school as a community of scholars, where some are teachers but all are learners.

Schools must begin to live up to their own stated purposes. The full range of sciences, arts, humanities, and social sciences should be the actual fare of a general studies curriculum offered to all children and youth and aimed at educating a free people.[1]

In this vein, we offer a vision of the best academic beginning for all the nation's schoolchildren based on four guiding principles:

1. All children can learn.

2. All children know something.

3. Teachers are central to students' learning.

4. *E pluribus unum*—out of many, one.

Though basic and seemingly axiomatic, these principles are frequently subverted in practice, as we shall see in our discussion.

1. ALL CHILDREN CAN LEARN

The suggestion that educators do not universally believe that all children can learn is bound to be greeted with impassioned denials and righteous gnashing of teeth. After all, the responsibility of their chosen vocation is the education of all children.

Perhaps educators do believe that all children can learn, but they do not believe they can learn the same things. Children identified as advanced are segregated from the mainstream into an academic elite. Although at the elementary level these children often remain in the regular classroom (with the exception of magnet programs), they are still treated to more interesting books and more challenging problems, and they frequently write and discuss material more than their counterparts. As researchers have discovered, schools extend considerable advantages to these children in the belief that they are smart and can handle it – the unstated complement being of course that the other children cannot.

Nathalia in Brooklyn

Happily, there are exceptions. During a visit to an elementary school in Brooklyn's District 15, we were treated to a classroom tour by a charming and articulate ten-year-old girl named Nathalia. The school she attends – situated within a larger, older school and drawing on the housing projects nearby – is only two years old and strives to incorporate the principles of the Coalition of Essential Schools.[2] As she showed us around her fifth-grade classroom, she explained the themes they were studying as a class (explorers, the colonial period), talked about the book they had just completed together about an African girl brought to America as a slave, and showed us some of the science research students were conducting individually. The walls were filled with colorful maps and graphs the children had made in cooperative groups that charted world explorations and immigrations to America, and collections of student essays were scattered about the room. Picking up one of these student books, Nathalia proudly showed us a bright and well-constructed essay she had written based on a folk story her Jamaican father had told her.

We were impressed with Nathalia and the class. Only later were we told that, until coming to this new school, Nathalia had been classified a "resource kid," meaning one eligible for special education. In fact, we found out that nearly 30 percent of the children in the older grades had been so classified. And yet by all appearances, they were happy — and more important, *learning* — in the integrated classroom. The methods of instruction and classroom structure used to accommodate diverse learning styles and abilities will be discussed in greater detail in Section Four.

We wish to stress here that even if children like Nathalia are not necessarily among the class's top achievers, they are still presented with the same learning opportunities — and they generally perform better than when in homogeneous low-level groups. Then with the benefit of an engaging learning environment, the Nathalias in our schools may well turn out to be high achievers themselves.[3]

Research again demonstrates two lessons. Individual children learn at different rates as they develop (a student who may be a bit slow learning phonics may yet become a fast and effective reader) and children are better at some subjects than others, or even at certain aspects within a particular subject. These findings do *not* justify the widespread practice of identifying certain young children as "slow" learners as though that were a predetermined conclusion and then isolating them in groups of similarly classified children along with the expectations their category implies. Rather, these findings point to the need for informed and sympathetic teachers to guide each child through different paths to the same goal. Granted, it is a tremendous undertaking, but it can be greatly facilitated by offering all children those maximum opportunities for learning such as would be found in an integrated classroom.

We recognize that at the extreme ends of the learning scale there are children who require special attention that

The continued abuse of classifying students as special cases contributes to inequity and violation of our first principle—that all children can learn.

may not be available in a heterogeneous grouping. These children, the severely learning-disabled and the prodigiously gifted, justifiably merit separate handling, and we do not include them in our discussion. However, the actual number of such children should represent a tiny percentage of all students. Certainly, it should be a much smaller proportion than that suggested by the current practice of identifying these children, which exceeds any reasonable definition of what constitutes the extremely learning disabled or gifted. To our minds, the continued abuse of classifying students as special cases contributes to inequity and violation of our first principle—that all children can learn.

Too many "identified" students

According to 1987 figures supplied by the Council of State Directors of Programs for the Gifted, forty-seven states support special gifted-and-talented education, sometimes called GATE, GT, or TAG programs, for their exceptional students.[4] Although one might imagine an Einstein or a Curie to appear once out of a hundred or even a thousand students, the national average of participation in GATE programs approximates 4 percent of all children in grades K through 12, with New Jersey leading the country at a whopping 9.9 percent.

Considering the sheer number of participants, it would be more accurate to call these children the bright and highly motivated instead of gifted and talented. Then we could see these programs for what they really are—tracking of the best students into the best academic programs, usually with better resources and teachers. Although this may be a nice perk for the children fortunate enough to be so classified (and typically for their high-achieving parents as well), it divests the rest of the students of the GATE kids' high-achieving example and the better teachers and resources. Worse, it honors a system of different expectations according to a child's preconceived ability, even when the children being classified are young and undergoing the mercurial changes and growth spurts typical of their age.

Special education programs, on their part, are becoming holding grounds for many children who could otherwise thrive in an innovative, integrated classroom. During the academic year 1987 to 1988, 7.2 percent of all K through 12 students qualified for federally supported assistance programs due to learning disabilities or speech impairment.[5] And this figure does not include children who qualify for local programs. Again, we recognize that some of these children need that individual, special attention. However, many that are currently enrolled in special education classes or pull-out programs would still be better served in heterogeneous groups. Despite the best intentions of teachers and parents or the efforts of federal policy to encourage mainstreaming slow learners into regular classrooms, odds remain overwhelming that a seven-year-old child relegated to low-ability reading and math groups, who may also spend one hour every week in a resource group, is never going to take calculus in high school. And that is *de facto* tracking of the most harmful and undemocratic kind.

Odds are that a seven-year-old child relegated to low-ability reading and math groups, who may also spend one hour every week in a resource group, is never going to take calculus in high school.

Alternatives to ability grouping

We are sympathetic to teachers who, wanting all of their students to succeed, feel compelled to give slower students extra time in resource groups or to remove them from competitive situations altogether. And considering the way most schools are currently structured, we can see how teachers could view ability-grouping as the lesser of evils. We have seen for ourselves, however, how the combination of a more fluid structure with different attitudes about children's capabilities works in integrated classrooms to the benefit of low and high achievers alike. Moreover, we have seen these classrooms in inner-city neighborhoods, in previously condemned buildings, with no resources, no libraries, and drawing on the poorest socioeconomic groups. And still the children learn.

Perhaps—and this is a highly qualified perhaps—teachers may find that certain situations require organizing children according to temporary difficulties with a

particular subject, for example, when confronting a class of six-year-olds who range from those who've never seen a book to proficient beginning readers, or teaching mathematics to an upper elementary class where some students are still struggling with division while others are tackling algebra. However, whenever possible, children, especially in the upper elementary grades, should be allowed to group themselves by their own interests and strengths. A group of children working together on dinosaurs – or even on beginning geometry concepts – because they are interested in them is a different matter from children forced into groups and excluded from some experiences by test scores.

Another alternative to ability grouping is to use the more advanced students to work with the less proficient students, as long as the advanced students' academic needs continue to be met. (This works especially well if the "tutored" child has a chance to be the "expert" in another academic area, for example, the struggler with math who is adept with languages.) Other classroom structures that work well to accommodate different levels of proficiency include flexible year-round school schedules whereas more time would be available to children who need it to master the material, or the organization of single classes for kindergarten through third grade and fourth through sixth grade in order to break open the artificial confines of grouping by age. A school in Louisiana is even removing grade barriers between grades in grades K through 5, thus obviating the threat of retention in grade.

Although we are arguing on behalf of equal, integrated classrooms, this does not mean that we insist on or even expect equal results from all children. Such expectations will almost always guarantee a curriculum watered down to a lowest common denominator. Children bring a variety of talents and interests to every task they undertake. They come to school in various stages of preparedness. However, schools must assure each student equal access to the best curriculum, resources, and teachers, regardless of a child's future potential – which is, besides, an extremely flawed prediction for educators of young children to make.

The fact that ability grouping often falls along racial lines makes this practice entirely reprehensible. Indeed, frustration with seeing available seats in academic classes perpetually filled with white students was one reason angry black parents in Selma, Alabama, demonstrated against the school board early in 1990 (an event that should also dispel the myth that minority parents do not value education).[6]

We believe that all children can learn. And we believe that all children can learn well enough that by the end of sixth grade they will, among other things, be ready for algebra and be reading a daily newspaper. Such is already the case in a smattering of schools across the country that significantly cross all demographic boundaries. To help all of the nation's elementary schools produce such graduates, educators must first be disabused of some commonly held misconceptions concerning the ways in which children learn.

2. ALL CHILDREN KNOW SOMETHING

The factory model for schooling also supports the fallacious assumption that children come to the classroom with empty minds waiting to be filled by teachers. An example of how this thinking has been constantly reinforced is the way reading is taught. Except for an impetuous infatuation with the look and say method and the bizarre hit-and-run appearance of the phonetic alphabet, reading is and has been taught by first learning that B is for buhh, C is for ssss and kuhh, etc., with the eccentricities of English vowels following close behind. Having mastered sounds and symbols, children are then typically treated to the banalities of Buffy the Panda and friends—the racially neutral but equally insipid Dick, Jane, and Sally of the late twentieth century. And so, children learn to read. Well, sort of. And therein lies the fallacy.

Having mastered sounds and symbols, children are then typically treated to the banalities of Buffy the Panda and friends—the racially neutral but equally insipid Dick, Jane, and Sally of the late twentieth century.

The fact that children do successfully learn to read with this method of first teaching phonics, then books, is not in question. However, the justification for a strict adherence to it *is* based on the false assumption that children confronting phonics for the first time in the classroom know nothing about reading. Actually the opposite is true. Some children, and especially middle-class children, (such as the Maintown child described by Shirley Brice Heath in "What No Bedtime Story Means: Narrative Skills at Home and School") come to school with the *idea* of reading already learned; although they do not know *how* to read, they know what reading is. This knowledge has been assimilated by being surrounded by printed language and books, by having been read to by their parents, and by watching grown-ups and older siblings reading to themselves.

When children lack the context of reading, the sounds and symbols of phonics are only disconnected letters on a page. To these children, phonics are not a means to an end (reading), but an end themselves, and as such, have no meaning.

When these children learn B is for buhh, they see it as a means to an end, the key to translating the mysterious symbols on the page into words, sentences, and ultimately stories. They understand without being told that by putting sound to symbol, they are making the first step toward entering the grown-up world of books. It is only because these children bring a preexisting understanding of the purpose of letters that the phonics first approach works.

This system breaks down when children come to school from backgrounds where the written word does not enjoy privileged status, like the African-American child in Trackton (Heath's fictitious name for the town). Three years ago, the Chicago *Sun Times* reported that about half of the five-year-olds entering kindergarten in Chicago did not know their last names, could not identify primary colors, and could not speak in complete sentences.[7] Such children are found in practically every urban school system in the country. Many inner-city and rural teachers tell of children who have never seen books or newspapers in their homes, whose only exposure to written language comes from television or outdoor advertisements. When these children are taught phonics first, they are almost destined to fail. Lacking the context of reading, the sounds and symbols are only that—disconnected letters on a page. To these children then, phonics are not the means to an end but the end itself. And as such, there is no personal significance attached to their mastery.

The best method for teaching children to read is to create a rich environment steeped in language and to teach phonics within the context of written narrative—simply, to start with something the children already know.

Begin with stories

The best approach for all children learning to read is to create a rich environment steeped in language and to teach phonics within the context of written narrative and story. Start with something they already know. Trackton children know stories, although they tell them in a way not acceptable to the school literacy culture. Elementary teachers must be sensitive and probing to find the appropriate hook to help such children grab the meaning of letters. The hook is there; all children know songs or have personal stories. The trick is to discover and build on what they know—what Pat D'Arcy calls using "the plankton-rich recall of personal memories and control language in all its forms."[8]

Our insistence on using stories to teach beginning readers treads on an emotional debate within the reading research community, the so-called "whole language" approach (essentially, the use of real books) versus phonics, as though the two need be mutually exclusive. The controversy is fueled by proponents from both sides who view compromise as weakening their respective approaches instead of strengthening them. Many phonics advocates still demand instruction in phonics through the sixth grade despite considerable evidence indicating that this prolonged approach has a numbing effect on children's desire to read. On the other hand, their resistance to change has not been aided by the few whole language proponents who believe that phonics should not be taught at all, and even that inferring the meaning of words in the context of the narration (e.g, reading "see" for "view") is as valid as "sounding out" an unfamiliar word.

The approach we promote neither emphasizes the discrete, prolonged learning of phonics nor dismisses the power of being able to translate symbols into words. Moreover, we do not view phonics and whole language as either dichotomous or sequential; rather symbol and word, word and story are mutually reinforcing and are best learned holistically.[9]

The fallacy of skills first, meaning after

The fallacy of phonics first, rather than phonics within the context of story, is representative of a larger pathology in the factory model school: the assumption that mastery of skills precedes knowledge of content. Typically in reading, this means that phonics leads to basal readers written in the stultifying formulaic prose of short sentences and approved vocabulary; real literature is the brass ring held out to those children tenacious enough to surmount the nonadventures of two-dimensional characters like Buffy and Mack. In mathematics, students are required to memorize number facts and multiplication tables before they are deemed ready to solve actual mathematical problems.

Another false assumption that pervades American elementary schools is that mastery of skills precedes knowledge of content.

A Poor Way to Teach Math

Susan Stodolsky comments on the conventional approach to teaching mathematics in *The Subject Matters:*

> The frequent practice in math of teaching a skill, providing practice with that skill in a predictable problem format, and then going on to another one is a procedure that almost guarantees forgetting and lack of connected learning. Students often learn "this page has problems to be done with this procedure" but do not develop a conceptual understanding that they can use in new situations.[10]

When business, industry, and postsecondary colleges and universities began to complain about the poor thinking and problem solving abilities of high school graduates, the educational research community came back with Higher Order Thinking Skills (HOTS). Programs in "thinking" were added on to the skills first content later (or never) curriculum, a solution much like trying to plaster over the cracks in a wall rotten inside with dampness.

Later research has established that what is called "higher order thinking" (as though this were thinking children must build toward) in actuality governs learning from the first. As Lauren Resnick says:

> The most important single message of modern research on the nature of thinking is that the kinds of activities traditionally associated with thinking are not limited to advanced levels of development.... [R]esearch suggests that failure to cultivate aspects of thinking such as those listed in our working definition of higher order skills may be the source of major learning difficulties even in elementary school.[11]

Resnick's list (widely cited and now all but universally accepted) describes thinking as nonalgorithmic, complex, yielding multiple solutions, involving nuanced judgment, applying multiple criteria, uncertain, self-regulating, imposing meaning, and effortful.

Children have been thinking since their first moment of consciousness, and from the age of toddling they have been learning to construct language with increasing sophistication. By the time they enter school they are usually speaking in reasonably well-conceived sentences—and can tell a pretty good tale besides.

Resnick's Definition of Higher Order Thinking

Lauren Resnick has found that higher order thinking actually governs learning from the first. She identifies key aspects as:

- Nonalgorithmic
- Complex
- Yielding multiple solutions
- Involving nuanced judgment
- Applying multiple criteria
- Uncertain
- Self-regulating
- Imposing meaning
- Effortful

Nevertheless, in the perverse manner of schools, spelling and syntax are taught as the precursors to writing, not as its refinement. But properly seen, grammar drills do not supply the material – the bricks and mortar so to speak – for expressing ideas. Rather, accurate spelling and grammar should provide the *finish* on children's language after the substance has been constructed. This also means that for younger children there should be considerable tolerance of spelling and grammatical "mistakes" in order to encourage them to express their ideas freely.

The misguided practice of focusing lessons on the discrete development of skills without content makes it difficult for children to connect their work to real learning. In addition, it unnecessarily wastes valuable classroom time that would be more efficiently spent advancing the whole class with mutually reinforcing lessons linking skill to content, and vice versa. The first recognition for teachers is that children enter the classroom with an abundance of raw material that can easily be augmented with more content and given form with skills.

Wasting children's time

The fallacy that children come to school knowing nothing is conspicuously manifested in what passes for social studies in the early grades. Known as "expanding horizons," this curriculum is based on a belief that children need to learn about the world beginning with what is most immediate and present – themselves – and "expand" their outlook from there. In "expanding horizons," children in the first three grades progress from learning about family to the school, the neighborhood, and the community – lessons that most children have been gathering on their own from age two or three.

A few years ago, Diane Ravitch, adjunct professor of history and education at Teachers College, Columbia University, and now assistant secretary in the U.S. Department of Education, looked into the origins of "expanding horizons" and discovered, surprisingly, that it has no basis in either child development or cognitive psychology. Furthermore, her survey of a dozen leading scholars in cognitive psychology, child development, and curriculum theory revealed that "[n]one knew of any research justifying the expanding environments approach; none defended it. All deplored the absence of historical and cultural content in the early grades."[12]

Despite this, it remains the prevailing curriculum in elementary schools, with the result that social studies is, says historian Charlotte Crabtree, "so thin, so skills-driven, so intellectually sterile and boring to teachers and students alike."[13] Little wonder then that by middle school, only 59 percent of polled students viewed social studies as "useful for my future" compared to the more than four-fifths who responded affirmatively about the usefulness of English and math (84 percent and 88 percent, respectively).

The persistent view that children know nothing—even about family and neighborhood—unless schools teach it to them is a gross underestimation of children's capacities. And remarkably for educators concerned with youngsters, it completely disarms children of their power of imagination. In *Teaching as Story Telling*, Kieran Egan criticizes the near-absence of history in the "expanding horizons" curriculum. Referring to what he calls this ad hoc principle of moving outward from "present, local experience to the unknown," Egan asks: "If this [principle] is true, how can we explain children's easy engagement with star warriors, wicked-witches, and talking middle-class worms?"[14] In asking, Egan's question answers itself.

History, replete with heroes, adventure, and far-away places, can captivate the imaginations of young children as easily as do fairy tales and legends. Yet its study is strangely absent from the early elementary grades.

But just as real literature is withheld until some arcane ability with skills is demonstrated, so is history as a discipline reserved for the upper elementary grades, by which time many children have been bludgeoned into indifference. The pity is that history, replete with heroes, adventure, and far-away places, can captivate the imaginations of young children as easily as do fairy tales and legends. But again, as with reading, what should be obvious to educators does not fit the factory model (or textbooks) and is considered too sophisticated for children who know nothing.

Among voices to the contrary, Egan and others rightly argue that stories – whether they be personal, fiction, or fact; printed, visual, or oral – should be central to the elementary curriculum, not some esoteric reward held out for demonstrated worksheet-and-drill proficiency. Engaging children's imaginations opens their minds to ideas and encourages them to handle more difficult material in ways not possible with dittos and textbooks written to formula. When reading a good narrative to themselves, they become motivated to read more and to stretch their own abilities. When listening to the teacher, they are learning to be more attentive, to discern and remember pertinent information, to anticipate where a story may lead, and to judge characters. Far from knowing nothing, children are in fact using critical judgment and abilities to synthesize and analyze material every time they confront a story – abilities that are sharpened and improved with each new tale. This is particularly true when the narrative is accompanied by class discussion or individual journal writing as will be described in Section Four.

The Faerie Queene in Virginia, 1990

During the last year we had the occasion to observe how story could be used in the classroom. We were visiting a class of third-graders in a public school in suburban Washington, D.C., where a parent volunteer of our acquaintance was telling the children the story of St. George and the Dragon as it was related by Edmund Spenser in *The Faerie Queene*. Her storytelling combined personal narration with readings from Spenser's poetry itself with a special emphasis for her audience of eight-year-olds on the "good parts" with monsters.

She introduced the Red Crosse Knight and Una and read of the encounter with the half-female/half-monster Errour "who spewd out of her filthy maw/A floud of poyson horrible and blacke." Quiet prevailed in the room, eyes widened. She continued telling and reading to them of the Dwarf and Archimago, of the heroes' vicissitudes, and of Red Crosse landing in the dungeon due to the treachery of the foul Duessa. She came to the part of an unknown knight coming to Una's rescue and hands shot up. "Is it Lancelot?" one wanted to know. "Nah. It's got to be Arthur," said another. After considerable discussion (with only a few, quickly suppressed unpleasant words between factions) and a search for clues in the passage just read, they continued with the story and discovered it was King Arthur indeed.

When finally they and Red Crosse had finished with "this the dreadfull Beast," the children asked if the story was true or legend, and they wondered and talked about what might have occurred a thousand years ago that inspired this story. After we left, the teacher had the children write thank-you notes, most of which included some rather imaginative artwork and all expressing their own opinions about this telling of St. George. Our acquaintance later shared these letters with us.

Many of the children remarked that they liked, as Kevin put it, "wen St. George saw the half women and half dragon that throws up." Sarah wrote, "The charecter I liked best was the dragon who throuw St. George in the well. I like old storys with dragons and monsters in them." And indeed, Sarah's letter included a rather accurately detailed drawing of Errour. In fact, most of the children's drawings, with smiling dragons no less, displayed an uncanny recall of the descriptive passages read from Spenser's poetry, more so than from the narrative "fill-ins." As vivid as Spenser's language is, we still were somewhat surprised that these non-GATE third-graders, or as a colleague calls them, JPKs (Just Plain Kids), did not feel intimidated by poetry that mystifies many college freshmen.

The moral of the story

The story of the Red Crosse Knight illustrates how children exercise the ability to reason and build on knowledge they already have. Both those who already knew of St. George and the Dragon and the ones who were merely familiar with the pattern of stories like this one were able to predict where the story was leading ("Is it Lancelot?"); they were able to make inferences about good and evil ("I liked St. George slaying the dragon."); and boys and girls alike identified with St. George (wrote Jackie, "that knight moth a bin a shog [strong] man.") Some even expressed a critical appraisal: "It was the asomeist [awesome-est] story I ever herd."

As these examples also suggest, the children's analyses revealed the development of other capacities, that is, the dimension that comprises the so-called "hidden curriculum" of moral education. These lessons are perhaps even less tangible than the ability to reason but certainly just as important to children's learning and development. For this reason, our agenda attempts to accommodate the moral aspect of schooling. Among the criteria used to select the stories cited in our literature section in Section Three we sought the capacity to convey good and evil, altruism and selfishness, philanthropy and greed, and the sense of choosing what is right between them.

The tradition of using literature as a springboard to developing moral sensibilities has fallen into disuse only during the last couple of decades. One of the seminal thinkers in child psychology, Bruno Bettelheim, had himself looked to fairy tales to foster children's moral development: "[The student] needs . . . a moral education which subtly, and by implication only, conveys to him the advantages of moral behavior, not through abstract ethical concepts but through that which seems tangibly right and therefore meaningful to him."[15] Bettelheim further wrote that "it is literature that carries such information best." We agree, which adds another compelling argument for the centrality of story in the elementary curriculum.

Meaning, first and last

Story is a concept that children bring to the classroom just as the ideas of reading or numbers are. Children's minds are *not* empty vessels waiting to be filled; they are rich with ideas, memories, and information, waiting for additions and shaping. By disregarding this fact, schools make learning more difficult than necessary for most children and nearly impossible for some. Most regrettably, the absence of story and content delays, if not discourages outright, children's development of reasoning, analysis, and moral judgment.

The absence of story and content from the early elementary curriculum unnecessarily delays children's development of reasoning, analysis and moral judgment.

In our ideal school, children will have been reading, writing, and discussing real literature and history, and they will be working with numbers in meaningful situations from their first day in the classroom. By the time they leave for middle school, they will be looking at texts more critically, they will be automatically drawing connections between new and existing knowledge, and their "moral compasses" will be sufficiently steady so that they can begin to infer and evaluate moral ambiguity.

These lessons do not easily fit into district curriculum guides, nor can they be evaluated by multiple-choice standardized tests. The demands of accountability frequently work against individual teachers' efforts at innovation and flexibility. But we know those teachers are out there.

3. TEACHERS ARE CENTRAL TO CLASSROOM LEARNING

Another notion that should be self-evident but is not is that the business of teaching and learning happens between teachers and students. Yet what, when, and even how students are taught is increasingly determined by higher levels in the educational bureaucracy. The regulation of curriculum and of textbook adoptions is usually governed by the district, county, or state. And although a sympathetic principal can be an effective buffer against the bureaucratic advance of regulation, all too often principals are themselves defenders of the status quo, whether it springs from a sense of conviction or resigned frustration. In any case, the rebellious teacher, like Lear, might just as futilely command the hurricane as defy district educational policy.

What, when, and even how students are taught is increasingly determined by higher levels in the educational bureaucracy.

Yet our agenda depends on teachers having the autonomy to be responsive to shifts in classroom dynamics and to be free to tailor lessons and class time accordingly. Curriculum guidelines should be just that – guidelines – not prescriptive, minutiae-obsessed manuals; textbooks should supplement not determine content.

The fact that a decade of legislated reforms – mandating increased quantity rather than quality – has failed to produce significant results in our schools shows that legislation will not in itself bring about necessary change in the classroom; it has in many instances restricted classroom learning. For example, the widespread mandate to cover an excessive amount of material in specific subjects ensures that *all* material will only be learned superficially. The bureaucratic fixation on specifics has further inhibited the free flow of ideas so important to students' development of reasoning and judgment. Mostly, top-down governance interferes with the creation of an environment where teachers and students can control the exchange of knowledge.

Unshackling teachers

Learning is not static; on the contrary, under the best conditions it is enthusiastically spontaneous and fluid. Teachers need to be freed sufficiently from outside constraints on classroom learning in order to harness this energy, both by guiding and following its flow. Part of this freedom must be extended to time – time for the class to reflect, to discuss what they know, and as a result, to arrive at new knowledge. In our setting, teachers wed lessons in content to students' reasoning, the ultimate goal being the reinforcing development of both knowledge and what are generically called "habits of mind" at Central Park East schools in New York City.

The Central Park East (CPE) complex in East Harlem is among the increasing number of rebel schools to regard these habits of mind as central to their educational mission. Consequently, their teachers are allowed the time and freedom to exercise their development in the classroom. Under the directorship of Deborah Meier, the

Five Habits of Mind

Deborah Meier and the faculty of the Central Park East complex of schools in East Harlem, New York City, regard the development of "habits of mind" as central to their educational mission. CPE students are routinely asked to analyze material for:

- Credibility
- Author's point of view
- Connections to students' existing knowledge
- Possible alternatives
- Relevance

These habits not only serve students' academic development, they form the bedrock of responsible decisionmaking for our future democratic citizens.

faculty at CPE lead children from the earliest grades to question, connect, and verify information, which develops their capacity for inquiry and judgment. By the time CPE students are ready for middle school, they have learned, as a matter of habit, to weigh new information and material for credibility, the author's point of view, connections to existing knowledge, possible alternatives to the material presented, and relevance. These five habits of mind do more than help children evaluate and build on subject matter. They prepare them for life in a world of mass media where the ability to discern bias and manipulation of fact becomes a vital part of responsible decisionmaking.

There is consensus in our society that a fundamental purpose of public education is the preparation of responsible citizens, including their development as future decisionmakers. Yet at the same time, we legislate more curricular requirements and demand more testing and accountability that serve only to strangle the very autonomy in the classroom that we wish our students to aspire to as voting citizens. We need to realign what we see as the democratic purposes of schools with how they operate in practice. This will entail allowing classrooms the freedom to pursue teaching and learning guided by national, district, and community objectives, not oppressed by their intervening regulation.

4. *E PLURIBUS UNUM*—OUT OF MANY, ONE

One out of many – the paradoxical tenet that we strive to embrace even as we wonder at its attainability. In constant search of balance, it seems as though the equation is always tipped either toward the one or the many. We are also aware that throughout our history we have fallen short of this ideal and frequently continue to do so. But as an ideal it is still something we as a nation invest in and work toward, even knowing that we haven't achieved it yet.

The reason we address "one out of many" here is that, as a democratic principle, it has direct bearing on the development of a philosophy for American public education. We see its influence in two distinct but related areas: first, as the American character values diversity, so should the schools inculcate in children a respect for tolerance; second, the school curriculum should accommodate and reflect diversity *and* a common culture.

The latter point has become an explosively sensitive issue over the last few years, for it touches on the sanctity of the "canon" – the collection of books that society values and, therefore, teaches – and efforts in academia to reexamine the historical record for unjust omissions. We believe that the move toward multiculturalism should be a shared goal for the nation of *e pluribus unum*. But regrettably, as with many educational issues that become politicized, the definition of multicultural has broken down into factions, each with a passionate attachment to its own agenda.

What we propose is an interim step even if not a complete resolution. Because elementary education deals with history and literature on a basic and general level, elementary schools offer a logical – and safe – place to introduce a multicultural curriculum and compromise on the fine points that have made this debate so divisive.[16]

Using students' heritage

For example, children's natural curiosity about people and different lands makes fascinating study out of tracing immigration from lands of origin into life in the United States. Our sample curriculum in Section Three sketches an interdisciplinary approach for students to research personal cultural heritage, whether this search takes a child to Norway, Vietnam, or Mississippi – or all three. There are many good biographies available for children about American heroes from Sacagawea to Lincoln to King, and a wealth of folk stories from Africa and Asia have been published for wider distribution. At the same time, American political history should be taught in a basic progression beginning with Native American cultures, and moving through English, French, and Spanish settlement to Jefferson writing the Declaration of Independence, George Washington taking the oath of office, and Lincoln emancipating the slaves.

An increasing number of American schools are fortunate enough to have a multicultural student body. In these schools, building on the backgrounds and stories that the children bring with them (see our second principle) can be a straightforward process. We recognize that some schools lack this ready resource; but a balanced and creative curriculum can still be developed by looking to the surrounding community and by the informed selection of texts.

We emphasize that building understanding and tolerance is an objective as necessary to the democratic imperative as all others discussed in this chapter. A program that attempts to bridge differences with knowledge must be part of every elementary school. Moreover, a truly multicultural program will honor the accomplishments of diverse cultures while demonstrating that individually they are, to use Diane Ravitch's metaphor, distinct threads woven into the fabric of the whole American culture. Again, the curricular specifics of such programs should be developed by teachers in response to the needs of the community and the goals of society; legislating curricula has an immobilizing effect

Building understanding and tolerance is an objective as necessary to the democratic imperative as all others.

on classroom learning no matter how laudable the intent.

Among our objectives for an ideal elementary school is that every emerging seventh-grader will appreciate both cultural and individual diversity and see it centered in the shared commitment to *e pluribus unum*. Our hope is that by secondary school, our students — *all* students — will wonder what all the fuss had been about.

Our basic statement of principles seems terribly remote considering the state of our public schools. But there is ample evidence — and we have witnessed it ourselves — that these principles can work and indeed *are* working in an increasing number of elementary schools across the country. There are other encouraging signs as well. A whole language approach to reading, based on phonics within the context of real literature, is rapidly being introduced in many school districts. Thanks to the efforts of the National Council of Teachers of Mathematics and others, doing real math to learn math is increasingly the method in many classrooms.

Yet these inroads, in truth, are few, given the thousands of districts and millions of students. The educational philosophy that we have articulated is the vital first step to ensuring that all elementary schools will be more democratic and more successful centers of learning. In the next chapter, we will see it working in practice.

NOTES

1. Haberman, "Thirty-One Reasons to Stop the School Reading Machine," 288.
2. The school and others connected with the Center for Collaborative Education are described in Anemona Hartocollis, "A Rebellion in Red Hook," 8.
3. Another example of inspired teaching and responsive learning is cited in Jonathan Kozol, *Savage Inequalities*, 47. In a broken-down and dispirited Chicago community, one teacher, Corla Hawkins, has a functioning cooperative learning classroom

full of stimulation for her fifth and sixth grade students.

4. *Digest of Education Statistics 1990*, Washington, DC: Department of Health, Education and Welfare, Education Division (USGPO), 65.
5. *Digest of Education Statistics 1990*, Washington DC: Department of Health, Education and Welfare, Education Division (USGPO), 64.
6. "Storm in Science," *American School Board Journal* 177, No. 6 (1 June 1990), 19.
7. "Chicago Kids in Crisis," series by William Braden, *Chicago Sun-Times,* June 26–30, 1988, specifically the article dated June 26, "Chicago's Underclass."
8. D'Arcy, *Making Sense, Shaping Meaning,* 6.
9. Anderson et al., *Becoming a Nation of Readers,* passim.
10. Stoldolsky, *The Subject Matters*, 113.
11. Resnick, *Education and Learning to Think*, 8.
12. Ravitch, "Tot Sociology," 352.
13. Crabtree, *Historical Literacy*, 187.
14. Egan, *Teaching as Story Telling*, 62.
15. Bettelheim, *The Uses of Enchantment,* 5.
16. John Pfordresher describes a healing approach to multicultural education in *Better and Different.*

1791
1865

SECTION THREE

WHAT TWELVE-YEAR-OLDS SHOULD KNOW AND BE ABLE TO DO

THE DETAILED list of knowledge and abilities that follows is subject to these important caveats:

1. Learning is multidisciplinary.

This curriculum is interdisciplinary. This should be kept in mind while reading these lists. The labels "literature," "history," "mathematics," and so on are artificial constructs for the sake of simplicity. But, for example, some of the books listed under literature may have been read in a history unit, and abilities listed under mathematics may have been developed in a science class.

2. Literacy is pervasive.

There is no reading or writing curriculum because these skills permeate the intellectual activities of the elementary school. Because there is no "reading" class or "writing" class, revision of writing, criticism of drafts, and production of final edited copy are all done within the context of the disciplines listed here or a combination of them.

SECTION THREE

WHAT TWELVE-YEAR-OLDS SHOULD KNOW AND BE ABLE TO DO

THE DETAILED list of knowledge and abilities that follows is subject to these important caveats:

1. Learning is multidisciplinary.

This curriculum is interdisciplinary. This should be kept in mind while reading these lists. The labels "literature," "history," "mathematics," and so on are artificial constructs for the sake of simplicity. But, for example, some of the books listed under literature may have been read in a history unit, and abilities listed under mathematics may have been developed in a science class.

2. Literacy is pervasive.

There is no reading or writing curriculum because these skills permeate the intellectual activities of the elementary school. Because there is no "reading" class or "writing" class, revision of writing, criticism of drafts, and production of final edited copy are all done within the context of the disciplines listed here or a combination of them.

literature of African-American children's classics (*Roll of Thunder, Hear My Cry* by Mildred D. Taylor, for example), but few parallel works have been translated from other languages. There is no doubt that this is a gap that must be filled. It is not a question of ignoring other cultures but of finding children's classic literature that represents them. Fortunately, the world's cultures are strongly represented in folktales, myths, and legends.

Our twelve-year-olds will have read classic children's novels of the kind we have cited. They will also know a wide range of poems and even be able to recite some of them. "Poetry" tends to mean lyric expressions of emotion for many teachers, but the genre includes heroic, epic, comic, and narrative verse, all of which are accessible to elementary students. They should enjoy Browning's *Pied Piper of Hamelin* and some of Tennyson's *Idylls of the King*, as well as Edward Lear's nonsense verse and Lewis Carroll's parodies.

They should also have read and acted in plays. There are excellent collections of scenes from Shakespeare as well as adaptations of children's classics. A teacher in a predominantly Hispanic school in the Los Angeles area introduces her students to *Romeo and Juliet* in the second grade. She tells them the story, has them memorize some important lines and present scenes to their classmates.

Stories, folktales, myths, legends

The stories that have formed the consciousness of human communities are the bedrock of literature. It used to be assumed that these folktales, myths, and legends were told to children in the form of fairy tales and bedtime stories, but we as educators can no longer count on this tradition for two reasons: children frequently have bedtime TV rather than a bedtime story, and the children in American schools come from such a wide variety of backgrounds and cultures that even if parents do tell tales to their children, a common "core" of stories neither can nor should be expected. It is therefore the business of the elementary school to give children knowledge of archetypal narratives.

These narratives are told among groups of people, have many versions, and embody themes that recur at all levels in literature. *King Lear* is based on a folktale, like many of Shakespeare's plots and subplots; St. George and the Dragon is magnificently dressed in the ornate poetry of Spenser's *The Faerie Queene* (as the children learned in the suburban Washington, D.C., school mentioned in Section Two); TV sitcoms have recognizable once-upon-a-time happily-ever-after plots. Here are a few of this genre of tales that the students should have heard by being told the stories, reading them themselves in modern versions, or hearing them read aloud.

Please note that this list is not definitive. These tales are not recommended above others, and because some do not appear on this list, this does not mean they are not important. The list is given only as a suggestion of the rich well of stories from which children should be able to draw.

- Aesop's Fables
- Anansi the Spider—An Ashanti tale
- Beauty and the Beast
- Grimm's Fairy Tales
- The Greek Myths
- Norse Myths
- Sir Gawaine and the Green Knight
- Legends and Folktales of Vietnam
- Paul Bunyan
- Zlateh the Goat
- Robin Hood
- The Crane Wife and other Japanese Folk Tales
- Bo Rabbit Smart for True: Gullah folktales
- St. George and the Dragon
- Arrow to the Sun and other American Indian Tales
- Aladdin and the Wonderful Lamp

- Baba Yaga
- Beowulf

In addition, we believe that stories from the Bible belong here as well because they are fundamental to the bulk of Western literature. There is no question of religious indoctrination, but to omit Biblical stories from the elementary curriculum means cutting off American students from the roots of much of their own literature and history, not to mention English, Russian, French, German, Spanish, and Latin American classics. To read Bible stories as literature is equivalent to reading the Ramayana, or even Greek tragedies, which had a religious significance at the time of their origin. The Adam and Eve creation myth can be read in the context of other creation myths from American Indian, Australian aborigine, African, and Norse legends. The tales of heroism and tragedy in the Old Testament's narrative of the conflict between the Hebrews and their enemies can be read in the context of similar epics. Depriving children of the story of Noah; of Joseph and his brothers; of Samson, Delilah, and the Philistines; of Job; and even of the story of Jesus Christ's birth severely cripples their later comprehension and appreciation of literature, art, and music, and also restricts their ability to understand social values and customs. The English language itself is permeated with metaphorical references that are opaque without at least an acquaintance with their Biblical origins.

Reading literature is basic, but reading must be accompanied by activities that develop students' understanding of its form and significance.

Understanding literature

Reading literature is basic, but reading must be accompanied by activities that develop students' understanding of its form and significance. By the time they graduate from elementary school students should be able to:

- Identify the genre and form of a piece of literature. Students should be able to look for the elements of a fairy tale (for example, the maiden rescued by a hero, the hero's journey, the hero's rejection and final vindication, the hero's ordeals, and the recurrence of events and characters in threes and sevens) and understand how they manifest themselves in specific works.

- Understand how narrative writing differs from the information delivery style they encounter in science, mathematics, historical, and geography books.

- Relate what they read to their own experience. Do they identify with the hero or heroine? Why? What would they do in similar circumstances? What lessons does the story have for personal decisions?

- Make reasoned judgments about the comparative quality of literature. Responses such as "I love this book" or "I don't want to read any more of this—I don't like it" are supported with analysis. Students understand that their reactions are a conjunction of the book's intrinsic features and the experiences that they as readers bring to it.

- Imitate each of the literary genres by writing their own stories and poems. Imitating them means understanding operationally the interaction between plot and character, the relationship between what the story is and how it is told, and the advantages and disadvantages of using a particular genre. They will have received discerning criticism, not undiluted praise, during the process of composition. The final products—both stories and poems—should be the outcome of repeated revisions (students tend to believe that the inspired first draft cannot be improved). Their stories and poems can be printed using desktop publishing programs, bound, and placed in the school library. Their plays can be performed by their classmates and videotaped for storage.

MATHEMATICS

Students graduating from our elementary school should be ready to study algebra. That is, by the end of elementary school, students should understand mathematics concretely and be ready to move into abstractions.

Students graduating from our visionary elementary school will wonder why people say they didn't like math in school and how these people can possibly seem proud of their innumeracy.

It is crucial that all elementary students, especially girls and minorities, be brought to the same high level of accomplishment and pleasure in mathematics. Research has demonstrated unequivocally that sixth grade is a watershed for ability to study science, engineering, and technology. Preferences are essentially set by the age of twelve, so that students without confidence in their quantitative abilities are unlikely to choose studies that depend on them.

Students graduating from our visionary elementary school will wonder why people say they didn't like math in school and how these people can possibly seem proud of their innumeracy.

These students will have developed the following:

- Number sense derived from years of experience with mathematical manipulatives.

- Operational sense, especially the application of operations appropriate to a given situation, such as whether to use a calculator or paper and pencil.

- Estimation as a guide to the appropriate procedure and the reasonableness of answers.

- Problem solving in realistic situations.

- Mathematical communication in the form of graphs, pie charts, diagrams, and written explanations.

- Mathematical reasoning based on concrete examples.

- Pattern sense so they can extrapolate from a small number of examples to a generalization.

- Data collection and organization.

- A sense of probability based on experiments with coin tossing, lotteries, etc.

- Spatial concepts such as area and volume based on concrete experiences and measurements.

- Ability to use computer programs that model situations using variables.

Above all, what characterizes our twelve-year-olds is an easy confidence in using mathematics in everyday life. They have always experienced mathematics as a way of understanding the world around them. They know why telephone numbers and car registration numbers have certain numbers of digits, why a large package of detergent is only cheaper if its unit price is smaller, how much carpet is needed to cover their classroom, and how much water is needed to fill the fish tank if it is 60 centimeters wide, 1 meter long, 75 centimeters tall, and 15 centimeters is to be left at the top.

They have compiled statistics on their class and entered them into computer programs, so that they have graphs, histograms, and pie charts about the national origins of the students; the number of girls and boys correlated with personal characteristics such as hair and eye color; and the distances they have to travel to get to school. They have hypothesized about the total amount of time the students watch TV aggregated together, and then verified their prediction by keeping individual records for a week and then combining them – again on a computer. They are familiar with scientific notation and proud of their ability to understand the relative magnitude of big numbers, such as the number of seconds in eleven and one-half days (one million, 10^6) as opposed to the number in thirty-two years (one billion, 10^9).

For elementary graduates, knowing and doing in mathematics should be inseparable from each other. They routinely write explanations of their approaches to tasks and problems and keep portfolios of the work they think best. Mathematics is a tool of thinking and also an end in itself—a source of pleasure and fascination.

Students will enjoy science in so far as they are conscious of it as a separate subject.

SCIENCE

By the end of elementary school, students should be ready to move into the study of science by disciplines, which may or may not be separated into courses. That is, they should be ready to study biology, chemistry, and physics, although in some secondary schools these will be interwoven thematically.

Being ready means having developed scientific skills and attitudes and comprehended scientific concepts. Students will enjoy science in so far as they are conscious of it as a separate subject. Both the scientific attitude and the knowledge they acquire will seem so natural to them that defining them apart from the rest of their knowledge will seem strange. Observation is needed as much in art as in science; hypothesis formation and checking is common to mathematics, history, and geography as well as science.

Skills and attitudes

Our elementary students have developed the following:

- Manipulative skills such as using balances, electrical testers, thermometers, and measuring instruments.

- Methodical observation, hypothesis formation, hypothesis testing, data collection, inference, classification, and explanation.

- Scientific communication in the form of research reports and visual displays like those learned in mathematics.

- A predisposition to question assumptions and assertions about the natural and physical world.

- Unwillingness to trust unconfirmed reports and naive explanations, even (and especially) their own.

- Cooperative working habits.

Concepts and themes

Our elementary students understand the following scientific concepts and can apply them:

- Cause and effect. "What makes this happen?" is a governing question in scientific research. From the time they can walk and talk children try to find answers to it. By the end of elementary school they should have experienced several situations in which they controlled the cause and documented differing effects, as, for instance, in growing plants under varying conditions or wiring an electrical device.

- Systems are cybernetic mechanisms relating causes and effects to maintain a balance. Students should understand such systems as the water cycle, food chains, and energy cycles in nature, and the principles of thermostats as they regulate heating and cooling systems.

- Scale fascinates children, who love stories about giants and miniature imaginary beings like fairies, perhaps reflecting their preoccupation with their own size in relation to the adult world. Their interest should be channeled into understanding what happens to volume when dimensions are doubled in size and what happens when they look at a bird from either end of a telescope. Clearly, scale is important for the understanding of maps and models, both of which twelve-year-olds should be able to construct with comparative ease.

ingredients
sequence

- Change is paradoxically a constant of nature. Like the other concepts we cite here, it surrounds us so that examples are available every second. Science teaching should provide students with ways of becoming conscious of change and documenting it. Observing where the sun sets or rises every day using a commonly known landmark; documenting the exact changes in the size, shape, and color of growing plant; or the stages of development from a caterpillar to a butterfly exemplify the experiences that twelve-year-olds should have had.

- Structure and function. "Why is this shaped this way?" is another question that children ask from the beginning. It applies equally to human-made objects (hammers with claws and hammers with balls, for example – why?) and to natural phenomena. Why are a cat's claws retractable? Why are the wings of slow-flying birds (and, comparatively, airplanes) longer and wider than those of birds that dart from tree to tree?

- Diversity as a principle contributing to the survival of ecosystems can be studied by looking at the variety of plants and insects that set up systems on waste city landfills or in a tide pool at the beach. The effects of difference on the system as a whole should be appreciated by imagining what the absence of one species would mean.

- Energy, its ultimate origin in the sun and the different forms it takes in nature, should be clearly understood as general principle by twelve-year-olds. They should know how food provides energy for them to move their bodies, and they should understand the analogy with the burning of gasoline in internal combustion engines.

Equipped with these concepts and skills, twelve-year-olds will all engage in a scientific experiment during their last year of elementary school. Unlike science fair projects that are usually voluntary and extracurricular, this experiment will be required of all students and will form the substance of instruction for at least a few weeks. While all students must take part, they can work in groups. They will formulate a research question, figure out ways to collect information, construct a hypothesis that explains their data, and then test it. There is no question of originality except to the students themselves: They must research something they want to know.

The experiment must be documented thoroughly, although the results can be recorded and manipulated on a computer. The results will be presented at a miniature conference where all the students from several classes (or perhaps from several schools in a district) present their findings. The experience of following the steps of a scientific experiment, even if the content is not sophisticated, prepares the students for the rigors of middle and secondary school science.

While gaining a firm grasp on chronology, students will understand history through controlling concepts such as migration; commercial networks; the building and decline of empires; political, social, and economic systems; and the leadership of great individuals.

HISTORY/GEOGRAPHY

Twelve-year-olds will be ready to study theoretical, even abstract, analyses of political and social events after experiencing history as a thrilling narrative taking place against backgrounds that shaped events.

In the early years of elementary school, students will have been introduced to history through biography and the stories that underpin our cultural history. They will have learned about the matrix of history by looking at families and communities changing over time. They will know about the diversity of people in their community, including the school. By the fourth grade they will have studied the geography and history of their own state.

They will also have begun the careful study of another culture, perhaps based on their family background or that of classmates. Such multicultural education is essential for children to better understand who they are, as well as to better understand – and not fear – the rich diversity of humanity. In addition, they will have moved into sustained examination of the chain of cause and effect that characterizes historical sequence.

By the time they graduate from elementary school, students will have studied both the major events of U. S. history and world history and geography up to the fall of Rome. The study of later periods and different areas of the world will continue in middle school and high school since the curriculum for history/geography continues through all twelve grades.

While gaining a firm grasp on chronology, students will understand history through controlling concepts such as migration; commercial networks; the building and decline of empires; political, social, and economic systems; and the leadership of great individuals. About the United States they will know:

- The detailed chronology of the United States from its beginnings through 1850 as basis for middle and secondary school study of later events.

- The political, social, and religious conditions in European countries that led to the colonization of America.

- The geography of the thirteen colonies and the beginnings of expansion across the Appalachian mountains.

- The causes, course, and consequences of the War for Independence.

- The establishment of the young nation's political institutions.

- The westward expansion.

- A general panorama of developments between 1850 and the present.

In world history and geography they will know:

- What the world looked like in terms of population density at major turning points in human history.
- Where and why civilizations developed and spread.
- The development of the great religions of the world and their effect on political and social events.
- The history of the Middle East, India, and China and their connections to Greece and Rome through trade in silk and spices.
- The extent of the Roman Empire, the reasons for its domination of the Western world, and its legacy to us now.

In the course of acquiring this knowledge, students will have learned to:

- Analyze the relationship of historical and geographical factors in major developments such as the rise of Mediterranean civilizations.
- Compare the features of different forms of society and government as they developed in ancient times and also as they contributed to the War of Independence in the United States.
- Realize that there are different points of view about the past and that no single view is necessarily right or wrong.
- Use multiple sources to research a historical period or event, including artifacts from the time as well as contemporary accounts and historical assessments.

- Imagine the past by enriching historical study with fiction, poems, plays, music, and pictures from and about the period or event being studied.

- Communicate, either in a group or individually, the results of historical investigation in a mock trial, simulation, or imaginative recreation of events.

- Given a sensitive presentation of both U. S. history and an unbiased survey of the early history of the world, students should be prepared to see in middle school and secondary school their own backgrounds and ancestors as the grand narrative converges on the present. They should be ready to understand the forces that brought them to their present homes and lives and begin to prepare for an active role in democratic society.

THE ARTS

Artistic experience and content have permeated the work our twelve-year-olds have done since kindergarten. Now they are ready with a body of knowledge to explore more deeply the art or arts they personally are attracted to as they move into a more abstract understanding of them all.

By "the arts" we mean visual and plastic art, music, theater, and dance. We have already spoken of children's experiences as creative writers under the heading of literature, but we could equally well subsume it here. As we pointed out, these disciplinary definitions are only convenient constructs.

Students will have had the following experiences in all the arts:

- Studio instruction. This means that they will not have simply been given permission to "express themselves" in paint, with clay, or in free-form dance. They will have been taught principles of drawing, musical notation, elementary stage-craft, and fundamental patterns and steps in ballet and folkdancing.

- Exposure to professional performances and exhibitions, with careful preparation before in the classroom and extensive written reactions afterward.

- Instruction in the history of art in the periods, times, and places they study in history/geography.

- Instruction in criticism and esthetics. Why do you think this is beautiful? Why does it move you? What makes one dance better than another, or one play more effective than another? What patterns can you discern in this painting or this piece of music?

- Experience in using technology for artistic expression, not merely to record performances. This includes electronic music (many students will have synthesizers in their homes), video and neon art, multimedia experiences, and performance art.

They will also have specific knowledge of each major art form:

- In music, they will be able to identify major differences in musical styles from different cultures, recognizing typical sounds and instruments; they will be able to characterize the major styles of European music, from the Renaissance through the great Romantic composers; they will be able to identify a symphony, a concerto, and an opera, and they will know the instruments of an orchestra.

- In visual and plastic arts they will recognize major stylistic differences between the major cultures, so that they could be expected to identify a Japanese landscape, a Native-American totem, and a Greek sculpture, for example. These will be tied to the world history/geography they have studied. They will also be able to recognize and place in the correct historical context the major trends of European art, such as Renaissance portraits, eighteenth-century landscapes, Impressionism, and modernism. For example, no student leaving elementary school should be ignorant of the *Mona Lisa* or Picasso's *Guernica*.

For the graduates from our elementary program, art is not voluntary or an add-on; it is part of the structure of their education.

- For both theater and dance, they should know the development of theater and its various forms, from the amphitheaters of Greece through the thrusting Renaissance stage to the proscenium of the nineteenth century. They should know what kinds of theatrical performances are characteristic of the civilizations they study in world history. Technology lends a hand here: videodiscs of extracts from Noh plays in Japan and Greek tragedies acted on their original stages should be available in the library.

- In dance, they will understand major styles and the body concepts they are based on – the extended toe of classical European ballet, the flexed foot of Hindu dances, the fluid rhythm of jazz dancing, and the percussion of tap-dancing.

The students' knowledge of and skill in the arts will be assessed as part of their integrated annual performances, but there will also be an annual concert and art fair to which all students must contribute. They may perform individually or in a group, they may present a piece from the musical or theater literature, or they may present their own original composition. Those who paint, draw, or sculpt may contribute the setting to a theatrical or dance performance, or may exhibit separately, or present their own performance art. For the graduates from our elementary program, art is not voluntary or an add-on; it is part of the structure of their education.

ADDITIONAL LANGUAGES

By the time they are twelve years old, students should be able to carry on a simple conversation in a language other than English. In many places there is a considerable variety to choose from in view of the immigration of students representing as many as one hundred languages in California, for example.

Lessons will be integrated into the life of the school—at lunchtime and during recesses—so that children learn to use the target language as a matter of course and also so that learning languages is experienced as pleasurable, not as a burden.

In schools where there is no sizable body of immigrant students, languages will be taught by native speakers of Spanish, Russian, Japanese, or Chinese. The lessons will be integrated into the life of the school – at lunchtime and during recesses – so that children learn to use the target language as a matter of course and also so that learning languages is experienced as pleasurable, not as a burden.

In those schools where there is a large population of speakers of the additional languages, students should be paired to spend time together. If possible they should be paired with such social compatibility that they will willingly spend recess time in each other's company. The children who speak the target language will be working with a bilingual teacher so that they learn English while participating in normal classroom activities. Practicing their native language with another student gives them the opportunity to maintain it and also to be honored in the school community for being an expert.

Approaching languages through conversation and normal everyday situations is consistent with research into the learning of languages. Researchers now recommend that additional languages should be learned as closely as possible to the manner in which a person's first language was learned – by using it to meet real needs. Total Physical Response (TPR) mirrors the development of language in children: They understand the words from the responses they evoke in others.

Research also points to the need for a "silent period" in which people presented with another language just listen to it. When they are ready, they will try speaking but cannot be forced. When they begin to use the language they depend on "comprehensible input" to keep moving them from the safety of what they know to new words and idioms. It is the teacher's job to provide the input that stretches the student's ability just enough without producing frustration.

Bilingual students are potentially sensitive peer tutors, since they have just been through the process of learning a language themselves. They have experienced learning English as a matter of necessity and understand the vital role of physical correlates and practical information.

The culminating performances at the end of elementary school will include an element demonstrating achievement in additional languages, perhaps with an explanation of the performance in the languages spoken by the parents of the students.

5

SECTION FOUR

HOW WE TEACH—THE CONDITIONS OF LEARNING

THE IDEAL PRODUCT OF ELEMENTARY SCHOOL

IDEALLY, A SECONDARY school teacher should be able to assume that entering students can read and write as a matter of course, and that they have been introduced to and are conscious of the different kinds of writing to be found in books on history and science (for example), as well as books read for pleasure. The teacher should be able to assume that students can write to support their learning, using journal entries and summary statements at the end of a class session, and that they can produce a simple but reasoned argument in a short essay.

Although it is not new to include thinking, problem solving, and reasoning in *someone's* curriculum, it is new to include it in *everyone's* curriculum.[1]

Similarly, a secondary teacher should be able to assume that students are able use the basic scientific skills of observation, inference, classification, explanation, and quantification, and that they can relate mathematical problem solving to understanding phenomena. Students ought to know the basic geography of the world and of the United States and should have a sense of major historical developments in the world—significant migrations of populations, for example—and in the United States.

What Secondary Teachers Should Expect

An elementary school education provides the necessary foundation for further study in middle and secondary school. Teachers of new seventh-graders should expect them to bring the following abilities and knowledge to their work:

- Ability to read and write as a matter of course.
- Awareness of different kinds of writing.
- Ability to write to support their learning, including journal entries and summary statements.
- Ability to produce a simple but reasoned argument in a short essay.
- Basic scientific skills of observation, inference, classification, explanation, and quantification.
- Ability to relate mathematical problem solving to understanding phenomena.
- Knowledge of basic geography of the world and the United States.
- Sense of major world and American historical developments.
- Basic knowledge of the components of culture.

Secondary teachers should expect that their students will possess a basic knowledge of the components of culture: the myths and fairy tales that undergird the world's literature and the different kinds of music to be found in different societies, and why they developed differently. Students might well be able to execute folk dances from other cultures they have studied, and they should have experience as discerning audiences of the arts, including theater, music, the visual arts, and dance. Students should have more knowledge of visual art than simple fun with paint. They should have learned the rudiments of drawing and of modeling, and they should have learned something about the criteria by which art is judged.

Other assumptions

An ideal elementary education would allow one more assumption by the secondary teacher: All students are able to express themselves in a second language. American schools now do not begin languages until it is too late to learn them easily. It is essential to restore additional languages to the elementary curriculum. At the moment, with few exceptions, only those children fortunate enough to have been born speaking another language and who have learned English in school have the advantage of a bilingual perspective.

The objective of elementary school education can be summed up as preparation for further study either of subject matter delivered in traditional divisions – chemistry, biology, algebra, English literature, American literature, and so on – or in broad curricular areas such as the humanities or mathematics and science taught together. Multidisciplinary areas in secondary education are by no means common, but they are beginning to gain ground in response to increasing awareness that artificial boundaries between disciplines are counterproductive in terms of understanding the world as broadly as we need to.

Some high schools in the Coalition of Essential Schools, such as Central Park East Secondary School in New York among others, already have broad curricular divisions. The graduates of our elementary school will be able to function superbly in such schools, which would be the ideal secondary followup to interdisciplinary elementary education, but they should have developed synthesizing habits of mind so well that they can work equally effectively in the rigid framework of traditionally separate disciplines.

Secondary teachers should also make assumptions about the conditions of learning in elementary school so that they can build on students' sound habits of mind.

Secondary teachers should also be able to make assumptions about the conditions of learning in elementary school so that they can build their disciplinary knowledge on sound habits of mind. The following are expectations of how children learn in good elementary schools.

1. BOOKS ARE THE CENTER OF LEARNING

Our twelve-year-olds will not only have read "real" books from the beginning of their school lives, they will also understand books as a major resource for problem solving. Encouraged to ask questions, they will be used to this answer from the teacher: "I don't know the answer to that question. Let's find out together. What books shall we look at first?" The students will use a library for information, ideas, and pleasure. The Vermont Department of Education expresses our vision as well as its own:

> There are no textbooks. But in most homes, and in every school room, there are books everywhere. Stop a young person on the street and jammed into ski parkas and hip pockets are cheap editions of excellent books. History, novels, classics, poetry, drama, humor, fantasy. Everyone reads.[2]

Because of their wide experience with reading good material (in our ideal world, basal readers and textbooks are things of an unregretted past), students write routinely; frequently, they write well. Since their early elementary school years, they have been producing their own books, now kept in the school library for the children coming into the school after them.

Because of this involvement with the written word in an intensely print-rich environment, reading and writing are not taught separately from other subjects. The disciplinary specifications we make in Section Three contain no lists of "skills" in reading and writing. These are assumed to be part of the learning of all the disciplines.

STUDY
AND BE A
GOOD
STUDENT!
AIR PATROL 101

2. LEARNING BEGINS WITH CONCEPTS AND INCORPORATES SKILLS

Children will not have learned thinking through add-on HOTS programs but will have developed their capacity to think by building on their innate desire to impose meaning.

Learning to read in kindergarten and first grade means, for these children, listening to stories and following the teacher's finger moving across the words in Big Books. Children need phonics and letter recognition *after* they understand why and what they are reading, and realize they need tools to get them to the meaning, as we explained in Section Two. Similarly, these students learn the relationship between addition and multiplication, subtraction and division, from manipulating blocks and tiles and groups of objects. When they learn the multiplication tables, they understand what they are reciting.

These are, of course, early grade experiences. Once in the upper elementary grades, they read books to enjoy narrative and to gain information. The students write their responses to the books' ideas as a matter of course. They learn the grammar and usage necessary to edit their work when they want to make it publicly presentable. They learn sentence structure and spelling at first by observing their teachers' written responses in their dialogue journals (the teachers are careful to use the same vocabulary in their replies) and from reading. In all cases, the desire to communicate meaning drives the acquisition of writing skills.

Students should have experienced learning as "Why?" and "How?" and "What does it mean?" not simply "What?"

Another example: In science, students understand some of the major natural systems (growth and reproduction of plants, the water cycle) from having worked directly with seeds or having modeled the relationship between temperature, clouds, and rain. From these experiences they have learned the scientific vocabulary needed to explain the processes. Since no one has erected artificial barriers between skills and content, they accept the complex interaction between them.

In general, they have experienced learning as "Why?" and "How?" and "What does it mean?" not simply "What?"

3. LEARNING IS INTERDISCIPLINARY

Connections should be made throughout the curriculum. As we have pointed out, reading and writing should take place only in a purposeful context — not reading for the sake of learning to read, but reading to learn history, or geography, or science, or for the pleasure of a story. Mathematics should be taught as a routine way of understanding the world by measuring everything in the environment, quantifying observed changes, understanding historical changes in terms of population explosions and decimations, and, of course, understanding latitude and longitude as the basis of geography. Artistic and cultural experiences are the essence of interdisciplinary studies — not frills added afterward or offered as rewards. A lesson in precise observation (seeing what is there, not what is expected to be there) will serve simultaneously as a lesson in science and in art. If the drawing of an object is followed by a journal entry describing the object in writing and a mathematics lesson explaining how to find its area and volume, then students are learning the language of different disciplines while integrating them by focusing on a single object.

Thus, learning through interdisciplinary themes or topics brings the conditions of learning to bear on what is learned. The object of all education is control over ourselves and our environment. Understanding the interconnections of subjects and at the same time the mental apparatus with which we apprehend them increases control. The world is not cut up into dry segments entitled "reading," "writing," "social studies," and "art," and children know this. A good deal of the present alienation from school is attributable to its artificial boundaries between subjects. This marks it immediately as a place unlike any other children experience and reduces its attraction as a source of excitement.

A good deal of the present alienation from school is attributable to its artificial boundaries between subjects. This marks it immediately as a place unlike any other children experience and reduces its attraction as a source of excitement.

An ongoing interdisciplinary project might be to have children understand their own personal histories by the end of elementary school. This would mean knowing where their families came from and why. In the case of African-American children, the forcible importation of their ancestors as slaves leads right into history, both U.S. and world history, and also into elementary economics and mathematics. All family stories lead back into geography and history, as well as literature, especially folktales, artistic experiences, and, in many cases, additional languages. While students begin to understand where they came from in time and space, they can explore scientific themes such as food chains and how they differ in different times, the water cycle and how different societies ensured access to water, and their own bodily systems.

Reading is obviously part of this "know yourself" project and so is writing. It is possible to spark early interest in linguistics by tracing the origins of family names. Each student might assemble a collection of products including essays and stories on the history of the family and the student, drawings and artifacts, numerical records of family members and their economic status (how much they earned in a Latin American country compared to their wages here, for example), even pieces of music on cassette tapes. All must be the student's own work, although the proportion of drawings to written material and numerical information will depend on the emerging capabilities and individual creativity of the child.

Using the student's own background to integrate knowledge is particularly suitable as a prelude to the intense self-examination and self-preoccupation of adolescence in the middle school and secondary school years. At the same time, however, students are learning to be successful social creatures. Sharing the fruits of their individual research and histories will build bridges and understanding to others. Furthermore, the importance of learning about one's own family and heritage should enhance, not diminish, the goal of diversity and understanding (*e pluribus unum*) outlined in Section Two.

4. LEARNING DEPENDS ON COOPERATIVE GROUPS AS WELL AS INDIVIDUAL EFFORT

As we argued earlier, elementary school should have no tracks, no groups of "fast" and "slow" readers, no "bluebirds" and "robins." All classes are heterogeneously mixed by ability and to some degree by age. There is one classification for grades K through 3 students and another for grades 4 through 6.

The most effective way of teaching heterogeneous groups is cooperative or collaborative learning. Students work together in structured ways on tasks that require the participation of more than one individual to perform them well. This is important: cooperative learning (like reading and writing) should not be done for its own sake; it must contribute to the successful completion of the task. Proponents of cooperative learning (Roger and David Johnson, William Glasser, and Robert Slavin) carefully emphasize this fact.[3] They also outline structures (the jigsaw, Student Teams-Achievement, Teams-Games-Tournament, for example) that control the process and ensure its productivity. They define roles within each of these structures, which teachers train the students to undertake. A wise teacher assigns roles after training and makes sure that each student experiences being the leader, the recorder, the researcher, and so on, before letting students follow their own preferences. Even when they do so, the teacher will ask them to switch roles if the group is not benefiting from their assignments.

The most effective way of teaching heterogeneous groups is cooperative or collaborative learning. Students work together in structured ways on tasks that require the participation of more than one individual to perform them well.

Cooperative learning requires a different attitude on the part of the teacher and therefore different training. Here it is worth noting that principals in California interviewing new teachers now ask prospective elementary teachers about their ability to teach using cooperative groups more frequently than any other experience or skill.

However, it is not always useful to work in groups, as the experts are the first to point out. And there are some students who by temperament and family background do not cooperate well. These students should be given the training necessary to work with a group if they have to for a given project, but they should not be coerced beyond being trained if they prefer individual learning.

Elementary school will give students some experience of all modes of learning, including lecture. Despite the "guide on the side, not a sage on the stage" doctrine, there are times when information is most efficiently delivered to a listening group, and students should not leave elementary school without learning how to concentrate, listen, and take notes. Even if the school rarely uses lecture, ordinary life presents us with situations—such as concerts or theater—where behaving with courtesy toward the performers and other members of the audience is necessary. And despite reforms at the K through 12 level, the lecture is still a primary mode of teaching in colleges and universities. Appropriate behavior in lecture situations is best taught and learned in elementary school.

Despite the "guide on the side, not a sage on the stage" doctrine, there are times when information is most efficiently delivered to a listening group, and students should not leave elementary school without learning how to concentrate, listen, and take notes.

In addition to heterogeneous groups within a grade, the elementary school will also form cooperative groups across grades. There are several excellent models of cross-grade clusters in elementary education, notably the elementary schools in the Coalition of Essential Schools and laboratory schools attached to schools of education, such as the Corinne A. Seeds University Elementary School at the University of California, Los Angeles, and the Bank Street School in New York City. A number of school districts have ungraded K through 3 classes. In Kentucky they have been mandated by new state laws required in response to recent court rulings restructuring the state school system.

Ungraded schools may employ teams of teachers to work with a larger number of students than in a "normal" classroom, thus permitting some specialization among teachers. One teacher, however, would be assigned as "anchor" for a small number of students. Within each cluster, students work in cooperative and collaborative groups whenever appropriate

Ungraded classes permit elementary students to develop at their own speed. They eliminate the threat of retention in grade, a punishment for poor performance that has been shown to have few beneficial effects and to increase greatly the chances of a student later dropping out of school altogether. Such classes also allow cross-age tutoring to take place within a single classroom. Cross-age tutoring has been shown to benefit the tutor (an older student) as much or more than it benefits the tutored child, but it is difficult to arrange in the traditional class structure where students must be pulled out from two separate grades and classes.

Cross-age tutoring has been shown to benefit the tutor (an older student) as much or more than it benefits the tutored child.

The social advantages of mixing grades and groups heterogeneously are obvious. Our point here is that they are also effective academically, and that more students learn better if they have experiences of working with others of different ages, backgrounds, talents, and kinds of intelligence.

5. LEARNING INCLUDES DISCUSSION AND CONTROLLED CONFLICT OF IDEAS

Socratic seminars, modeled on the ideas of the Paideia Group, allow students to practice in small groups the language of academic discourse.[4] Ideas become palpable; arguments can be mounted and challenged; students learn to listen and to speak, to fashion thoughtful responses, and to critique themselves and others. They actively participate in discussions of texts and works of art in regular seminars, so that they begin to understand ideas and values and how these may often come into conflict constructively. Socratic dialogue enables students to see how ideas are shaped and reshaped in an atmosphere where all participants are respected and all ideas are subject to question. Students discover for themselves that the arena of ideas can be a battleground of competing conceptions, but this constructive conflict is central to the democratic tradition. They also find out that there are no easy answers to many of the most important questions—certainly a conclusion to be expected from Resnick's characteristics of thinking, which are listed in Section Two. Since thinking involves judgment, and judgment must ultimately be trusted, it must be developed and strengthened by soundly based argument.

Students discover for themselves that the arena of ideas can be a battleground of competing conceptions.

6. LEARNING AND TECHNOLOGY ARE INSEPARABLE

While books are the central technology of education, our twelve-year-olds will have lifelong familiarity with the tools now indispensable in the worlds of business, industry, government, and research. Computers will be so completely accepted in the classroom as to become part of the background. They will be used for the following:

- Modeling in all subjects so that students understand the use of variables and the effects of changing them.

- Word processing. Writing will be routinely produced on the word processor so that students can revise constantly. Students will use spell-checking programs so that their attention is not distracted from the rhetorical effects of their writing to less central matters.

- Communication with the teacher and with other students in the class so that the teacher comments directly on a student's writing and can also direct another student to look at the comment instead of writing it again. This network, of course, applies to all the subjects.

- Communication by modem to other schools, near and far, to correspond with other students as colleagues and equals in the quest for learning, thus reducing xenophobia and prejudice through familiarity.

- Accessing data bases and library catalogs to enrich research.

In addition to computers, calculators will be the expected tool of mathematics. Students will have used them since their first days in school. Since calculators have been commonplace tools of the classroom throughout their school lives, our twelve-year-olds will be sophisticated about them and about their limitations.

It is important to point out, however, that the use of calculators does not necessarily mean that students will be able to study more advanced mathematics at an earlier age. Cognitive development imposes boundaries for most students. What the use of calculators will produce within the context of conceptual mathematics instruction will be students who are confident of their mathematical understanding and reasoning. "Math anxiety" should be a forgotten neurosis, especially among girls and minority students.

Accompanying computers and calculators will be video technology of all kinds. Videodisc players will enable students to review information they feel insecure about or to watch scientific experiments or processes that otherwise could not be brought into the classroom. Videotaping student performances will be routine, and the technicians will be the students themselves. Schools will send home videotapes as part of their quarterly report to parents. Students will use interactive computer-video links for help with research or homework.

Just as books are sources of both information and pleasure, students will enjoy computer and video games. They will have learned criteria for judging their quality just as they have learned to evaluate books, music, pictures, and plays.

The National Council of Teachers of Mathematics on the Use of Calculators

The National Council of Teachers of Mathematics (NCTM) supports calculator usage in its standards for K through 4 mathematics as described here:

> Calculators enable children to explore number ideas and patterns, to have valuable concept-development experiences, to focus on problem-solving processes, and to investigate realistic applications. ... Calculators do not replace the need to learn basic facts, to compute mentally, or to do reasonable paper-and-pencil computation. Classroom experience indicates that young children take a common-sense view about calculators and recognize the importance of not relying on them when it is more appropriate to compute in other ways.[5]

7. LEARNING OCCURS IN DIFFERENT WAYS AT DIFFERENT SPEEDS

Our twelve-year-olds will have roughly the same preparation for middle school and secondary education, but it will have been acquired according to their individual learning styles.

Some students will need special help. Students speaking another language who enter school in the upper elementary grades should be taught, where this is possible, by bilingual teachers; their primary language should be the medium for learning, so that they do not fall behind in academic subjects while learning English. While they may not completely command English when they graduate from elementary school, they should be at the same level as their classmates in mathematics, history, geography, science, and art. As we just pointed out, these bilingual students do not need to learn an additional language. Indeed, they should be encouraged to help classmates learn their language.

The case is similar with disabled students, those whose disabilities do not preclude them from participating in the mainstream classroom. Technology is immensely important for them. With its help, and with additional tutoring where necessary, disabled students can learn at appropriate speeds but arrive at the same results as their classmates.

Multiple Intelligences

Harvard University researcher Howard Gardner identifies seven modes of intelligence that appear in varying proportions in different students:

- Linguistic
- Musical
- Logical-mathematical
- Spatial
- Bodily-kinesthetic
- Interpersonal
- Intrapersonal

According to Gardner, these intelligences determine in part the way individual children learn.

However, the point is even more general than insisting that different languages and different physical conditions are not barriers to learning. Howard Gardner has postulated seven kinds of intelligence—linguistic, musical, logical-mathematical, spatial, bodily-kinesthetic, interpersonal, and intrapersonal—that people may possess in varying degrees. It is clear that traditional education has valued linguistic and logical-mathematical ways of apprehending the world almost to the exclusion of the others.[6]

When students graduate from our ideal elementary school, they will have experienced teaching and learning in all the modes of intelligence. If one mode seems to predominate in the child—the spatial intelligence of a painter, the musical intelligence of a composer or performer—that will be honored equally with linguistic and logical-mathematical intelligence. Matches between the intelligence of the teacher and the emerging intelligences of the students cannot be expected to be perfect. It is essential for teachers to understand that some students learn best by listening, others by seeing, and some through bodily movement. The speed and mode of learning will vary as these intelligences manifest themselves, sometimes singly, sometimes in combination. These natural developments will have been noticed by teachers who will have adapted their instructional styles to accommodate the students' different—but equally valuable—intelligences. They cannot teach to all students in all styles at all times, but they can teach in each style some of the time.

8. ASSESSMENT SERVES LEARNING

The assessment of our ideal elementary program is characterized by respect for judgment—the teacher's own judgment, the students' developing ability to monitor their own progress, and the collective judgment of professionals. There is no attempt to reproduce the spurious "objectivity" that has led to norm-referenced, multiple-choice testing with its destructive effects on curriculum and teachers' morale.

Such a bald statement may need some amplification. Machine-scorable testing arose from the same misconceptions that supported the factory model: Teachers could not be objective in judging their own students because that was not their job. They installed the screw, they didn't inspect it. Knowledge is the same thing as fact, so test fact and you'll assess knowledge and understanding of it. The curriculum can be divided into discreet bits of knowledge, making "items" easy to devise. Efficiency is the main criterion, so the form of the test must be machine-readable to process large numbers.

All of these misconceptions have proved to be destructive to good teaching, although perhaps the form of the test – bubbles to be filled in with number 2 pencils – is most visible as a crippler. Intended originally as an efficient proxy for learning, the discrete items became ends in themselves. Children are drilled in terms of choosing a,b,c, or d even when reading, so that they will be ready for the test. To score high on the test, children have to understand both the test directions and the mindset behind the limited choices.

There are defenders of multiple-choice testing who say that items can be designed to avoid these inanities and even to assess creative thinking. While that may be so, there is no denying that whatever the virtues of the item, the response is passive recognition. The student does not have to write or otherwise engage actively in the mental and physical behavior that we want to see in our students. We listed the characteristics of thinking in Section Two. They do not fit the straitjacket of multiple-choice items.

A word about "objectivity." The only process that may be so described is the machine-scoring itself. Everything else in the production of norm-referenced, machine-scorable, multiple-choice tests is as subjective as anything is in human life – but the fact is not well known. Tests are developed in publishers' offices by experts whose priority is psychometric soundness. If a field or pilot test shows that too many children get the

What's Wrong with Multiple Choice

Here is an egregious example.

> Sample: Find the sentence that has the words in the correct order among "A boy walks. Walks a boy. Boy walks a." "There's two of them," said Marie. "Show me," said the administrator. She pointed to the first two. "Where have you seen a sentence like the second one?" asked the administrator. "At the video place—*Comes A Horseman*. Have you seen it?" "Yes," he mused, "it's one of my favorites."[7]

answers right, those questions are eliminated. Consequently, the material tested is unlikely to be the main concepts of a topic, but peripheral, even trivial items. The concern is to spread the scores out along a bell curve, *not*, as many people think, to ascertain how much children know.

There is a movement rapidly gaining strength to replace norm-referenced, machine-scorable, multiple-choice tests with assessments called "alternative," "authentic," or "performance," although all the terms refer to the same genre of assessments. Some states have already adopted performance assessments for their statewide assessments. A statement from the California Education Summit in December 1989 called for an end to multiple-choice testing "because of its deleterious effects on instruction."[8] In May 1990, the National Commission on Testing and Public Policy issued *From Gatekeeper to Gateway: Transforming Testing in America*, which recommended that "Testing programs should be redirected from overreliance on multiple-choice tests toward alternative forms of assessment."[9]

Our ideal elementary school eschews multiple-choice tests for these reasons. It uses performance assessments because they can be folded into the regular routine so that students cannot tell when they are being assessed. Student progress is assessed mostly by portfolio and teacher observation. Students keep their work in individual and group portfolios, maintaining complete records of all the stages in its preparation. They also have sets of diskettes and videotapes of presentations.

At specified times during the year, the teacher will ask them to look over their work and choose what they think is best according to a clearly stated criterion. Perhaps the teacher will ask them to select those pieces (print or electronic) that the students think show greatest improvement over previous work, or to choose work that the students think is most daring and shows most originality. Students may work with their cooperative group to get their advice about choosing pieces, or they may discuss their choices with a teacher. They thus have an opportunity to reflect on their own progress and to consider what they have achieved and what they need to address now. The teacher may ask the students to go back to an early piece and revise it some months or a year later so that they have a clear sense of the difference in their development.

These portfolios and the opportunities they give students to assess themselves are the backbone of student evaluation. They provide teachers with the information they summarize for parents in periodic reports. These reports have no grades, only checks against the level of progress – outstanding, satisfactory, needs improvement, unsatisfactory – and narrative explanations.

Teacher observations may be formalized or guided by using the Primary Language Record (PLR), developed in London elementary schools to communicate teachers' observations to parents, administrators, and interested authorities. The PLR consists of two forms: one, a record which follows child throughout a school year and is handed on to the next teacher; and the other, a form for teachers' notes and observations. Both become the basis for the narrative reports to parents. The distinguishing feature of the year-long record is an initial interview with the student's parents about the child's literacy interests – what the child likes to read, draw, write, watch on television, and so forth. No judgments are made. The parents' responses are summed up by the teacher on the form, and the parents read the summary (or have it translated for them if they are non-English speakers) and sign it.

The interview represents a cooperative approach to working with parents. Too often, especially among immigrant and traditionally working-class parents, the expectation of talking to a teacher is that the parents will be made to feel guilty about the behavior of their children. Cutting across this expectation, teachers using the PLR ask (not tell) the parents to help the school work with the child.

Teacher observations need not be onerous: the form is provided so that only a few words in the relevant spaces will record information. About three times a year, the progress of each child (sometimes one out of thirty-eight in an inner London primary school) in reading and writing will be individually assessed. The child is asked to choose a book and read to the teacher, who comments on progress in terms of the child's understanding, ability to deal with unknown words, and ways of going about the task of reading. Writing samples are kept with the record so that it can also act as a portfolio.

The PLR is currently being adapted to cover progress in mathematics and science.[10] It is gaining increasing attention in the United States as it becomes clear that so-called "objective" tests give little useful information to teachers or parents about the child's accomplishments. The factory model of schooling excludes teachers' judgment, since in the model teachers have the role of technicians who need to be closely watched to ensure performance. On the other hand, in a community of scholars, teachers' judgments are valued but also bolstered by cross-checking with colleagues and with the principal.

Most importantly, the teacher's observations and frequent conferences with parents are only the surface features of an ongoing assessment process taking place continually between the teacher and the students. It is the teacher's objective to make students responsible for evaluating their own performances, so teachers repeatedly ask: "What do you think of this? What are you most pleased with? What could you have done better?" Self-assessment is ultimately of greatest value to students as they move toward control of themselves and their environment.

However, once a year the programs of instruction at each level – lower (K through 3) and upper (4 through 6) – are assessed by the state for the sake of accountability. Since this is strictly a program evaluation, there is no need to test each student individually. While it is perfectly defensible to assess programs by matrix sampling (students write essays and a sample is holistically graded, for example), it is also possible to assess programs by group performance. This is no burden for either students or teachers since it becomes an opportunity to display accomplishment.

In our ideal elementary school in our ideal state, the program assessment at the elementary levels is interdisciplinary, like the instruction. The state assigns several topics so that groups of students in a grade level can work on different subjects. For example, one group might be assigned to produce a videotaped news broadcast with all the information needed to report on one day in history. Another group might be asked to produce a collective report on bridges, their history, construction, and variety. Another might be asked to prepare an advisory report on the location of a park in a hypothetical city. All the presentations must include artistic production of whatever kind is appropriate to the topic, and all must include the use of additional languages, perhaps a description of the presentation in the languages of the immigrant parents in the audience.

These tasks should be part of the normal instructional program in elementary school. The distinguishing feature is only that when they are presented (as all group projects are presented) to other classes, teachers, and parents, also among the audience are three state-designated evaluators. These are teachers from other schools in the district who have been trained at the state department of education with representatives from all the other districts in the state to observe and score the school's accountability performances. They have checklists for the features to be included with scales for the quality of the features, but they are also trained to give a summary score based on their collective judgment and training.

Thus the public is certain of receiving reliable information about the quality of programs in the schools, and—what is more important—the school's program is not disrupted for assessment.

NOTES

1. Lauren Resnick, *Education and Learning to Think*, 7.
2. Vermont Department of Education, *Should These Be Vermont's Goals for Education?*, 3.
3. David W. Johnson and Roger T. Johnson, *Learning Together and Alone*; William Glasser, *Schools Without Failure*; Robert E. Slavin, *Cooperative Learning: Theory, Research and Practice*; and Slavin, *Using Student Team Learning*.
4. Described by H. Dennis Gray, *Socratic Seminars,* and in "Putting Minds to Work," *American Educator,* Fall 1989.
5. National Council of Teachers of Mathematics, *Curriculum and Evaluation Standards,* 19.
6. Gardner, *Frames of Mind,* passim.
7. Dorothy F. King, "Real Kids or Unreal Tasks," 6.
8. *California Education Summit Final Report*, 17.
9. National Commission on Testing and Public Policy, *From Gatekeeper to Gateway*, 6.
10. An adaptation called the California Learning Record is being tested in California, New York, Alaska, and Hawaii as a model for the assessment of compensatory education (Chapter One) programs.

STAIRWAY

SECTION FIVE

LIFE AND CULTURE IN THE ELEMENTARY SCHOOL—A PORTRAIT

THE BUILDING is dirty brick, old and uninviting. Across the asphalt yard solid metal doors present a forbidding front. There is no handle and the juncture of the doors is covered with a strip of metal to protect the locks. It is necessary to knock so that someone inside can push the door open.

The noise immediately overwhelms as the visitor signs a book at the security desk. The noise is predominantly laughter and the sound of running feet bouncing off the stone walls and high ceilings. Noise turns out to be a constant of life in this school, a nerve-scraping reminder that schools were once physically as well as organizationally built on the factory model.

But the dingy block walls are bright with large paintings of clearly imaginary scenes since there are blue figures, bright yellow houses, and spotted landscapes. In the corridors under these paintings are little groups of children, some accompanied by adults around tables, others sitting beside each other on low chairs with books and notebooks open on their laps. Looking into open doors, the visitor finds it hard to continue walking down the corridor. The rich clutter of charts, drawings, and lists on the walls, the children's papers strung across the

Noise

The most immediate difference that strikes the observer between an energetic elementary classroom and one based on the factory model of education is the level of noise. This may disconcert those who remember classrooms where quiet was equated with academic study, as it did us on our first visit to a school in the Red Hook section of Brooklyn. However, it soon became clear to us that the noise was actually the refreshing sound of children in active engagement with math and science projects or eagerly expressing opinions in class discussions. As we show in this section, qualified teachers can effectively manage the activity and accompanying noise, keeping all children on task.

room on suspended strings lure like the Sirens' song. From inside the rooms, intriguing noises compete with the clatter in the hallways.

But the visitor needs some background to understand what is going on. This is a building in any urban neighborhood in the United States, long out of date but still

Schools within Schools

New York City's School District 4 located in East Harlem is the success story most frequently cited by the supporters of school choice, an issue that will be discussed later in this section. But in addition to choice, one of the greatest lessons gained from the District 4 experiment is the distinction between *school* and *building*, entities that don't necessarily have to be the same.

Many of the country's elementary schools, housed in large, postwar buildings accommodating as many as one thousand or more, can be cold and intimidating places for our younger students. In these impersonal surroundings it's easy to lose track of children, especially those who possess neither the strength of personality nor a proclivity to cause trouble that will get them noticed by the adults in the building. Furthermore, the academic management of such a large student body almost demands fitting the student to the established assembly-line mode, rather than adapting an instructional program to meet the needs of the child.

In our portrait, the four separate elementary schools contained in this single building offer both the intimacy children need to avoid feeling like anonymous cogs in the factory machine and a variety of instructional programs from which parents have the freedom to choose.

used and not regarded by those who work in it as a serious obstacle to educating children. Similar buildings can be found in diametrically opposite situations, such as schools on Indian reservations in the Southwest.

The building we are focusing on can accommodate about one thousand children, but it divided into four separate elementary schools. There are actually five physical parts to the school, for one section of the building is set up as a before- and after-school daycare center. The five parts all share one library, but otherwise, facilities are self-contained, including fenced-in asphalt recreation areas like the one the visitor crosses on the way in.

A Community Center

The mission of schools must be students' academic development. Nonetheless, it is painfully clear to many educators that the emotional and physical needs of an increasing number of students erect perilous obstacles to their ability to learn. It is equally apparent that teachers cannot by themselves take on the responsibility for students' mental and physical well-being in addition to the sufficiently difficult task of educating them.

For this reason, many urban school districts have reached out to area social services with plans designed to connect their programs with the schools' students and families. Just as the existence of a building no longer has to represent a single school, neither does it have to contain purely educational services. By viewing the school building as a community center, it is possible to deliver social services more effectively and efficiently to those who need them most. Programs to provide comprehensive services to children and their families have already been initiated across the country, notably in San Diego and Savannah, Georgia.[1]

Each of the self-contained elementary schools has its own staff of teachers, administrators, and auxiliary personnel. These include social service coordinators who maintain children's health and welfare by working with federal, state, and local agencies. Having welfare coordinators assigned to each school maintains the atmosphere of a caring family. Help is available within each school unit for homeless or abused children and for those who may need special services to overcome a physical or mental disability. We find out during conversations that the social service coordinators work closely with families on all aspects of children's development, not only their progress at school.

The building supervisor, ultimately responsible for safety in the building, is located in the daycare center and has no authority over the four principals for the internal conduct of their schools.

This school building is open every working day of the year from 6:30 A.M. until 7:00 P.M. Children may breakfast in the daycare center and read or play until their school opens at 8:00 or 8:30 A.M., depending on the schedule that the school's personnel find congenial. After school, children may play on the playgrounds under supervision, read in the library, continue their work at tables in the daycare center or on the computers that line the walls of one room, listen to stories read by volunteer high-school students, or go by bus to a nearby park for supervised games. Tutors, some of whom are older students, are available for children who wish extra help.

The school's year is divided into four quarters: September through December, December through March, March through June, and June through September. The work is designed so that students can complete preparation for middle or secondary school by attending three out of four quarters—even by keeping strictly to the traditional September through June schedule. Some

Year-Round Schools

The year-round school is the one concept in our portrait with the least precedent. There are schools, for example, in Los Angeles and San Diego, that are open twelve months but only to alleviate overcrowding. Students continue to attend for the standard nine months. The idea for year-round schooling is gaining credibility, however, as more serious discussion is given to such matters as a 220-day school year and opening the school building to the community. Under this system, the stigma of attending "summer school" would disappear as the distinction between school and community services becomes blurred.[2]

students take advantage of this option. Since the school spans the socioeconomic spectrum, there are students who accompany their parents on extended foreign travel for business or academic reasons; others expect to spend the summer in camp or on farms.

However, the majority of students attend school for all four quarters and take time off when their parents have vacation. Attending school for four quarters may be related to a student's progress, but it is essentially a matter of discussion between the teachers, the parents, and possibly social welfare coordinators in the case of children needing special services. Attending for four quarters means that the slower students will achieve the results we outlined in Section Three; they will be prepared for deeper, more abstract study of the basic academic subjects. Students who have arrived at the same academic level in less time can explore other areas with the help of the librarian and teachers. For example, they may learn the history and geography of Latin America, construct scale models of real or imaginary buildings, develop multimedia art performances, learn computer programming, or devote themselves to tutoring other students. In no sense are some children receiving more opportunities than other children; the scheme simply takes into account their different learning styles and speeds. It is of paramount importance that all the students will, for example, be ready to start algebra when they go to middle school, and the school's main resources are devoted to this end.

All of the schools are racially and ethnically mixed as well as socioeconomically. Parents choose a school on the basis of personal preference for one group of people, schedule, and emphasis over another. All parents in the district must choose, just as they will choose secondary schools with special programs in quantitative subjects, humanities, and arts in consultation with their children and their children's teachers. They choose a school within the parameters of racial and gender balance and an upper limit on numbers. Choice means that parents must devote some thought—however little—to what

Choice[3]

School choice is high on President Bush's educational agenda and, according to a recent Gallup Poll, enjoys general public support.[4] The theory underlying choice is that the effectiveness of a school will increase when teachers, parents, and students share a sense of ownership in its mission by choosing to attend it. Beyond this simple definition, however, the models of school choice are probably more varied than the options they are supposed to offer. These plans range from Minnesota's optional open enrollment to Cincinnati's magnet schools to Milwaukee's authorization of vouchers to disadvantaged families that can be redeemed at nonpublic institutions. The only common thread through all of these plans is the requirement that racial and demographic balance be maintained. Predictably, the results are mixed.

Our portrait is based on the models in Cambridge, Massachusetts, and New York City's District 4 in East Harlem. The following elements contained in these districts contributes to their success:

- *Choice is restricted to the public schools.* Allowing parents to take vouchers to nonpublic institutions raises constitutional questions in regard to parochial schools and opens legitimate concerns that exclusionary policies in certain

they want for their children and whom they trust to care for their children for the majority of their waking hours. It increases the probability that parents will involve themselves with the school.

Each of the four schools in the building is small enough for all the staff and most of the students to know each other and even their families. Children with special needs, such as children who enter not speaking English, are treated carefully, without drawing attention to their condition. They may receive tutoring during school or in the daycare center, but the stigma of the pull-out is avoided. In any case, as we shall see, there is so much variety of activity in the classroom that it would be hard to see who is pulled out and who remains.

Now at last we can go into a classroom. We are looking at a class of eleven- and twelve-year-olds because we want to see how they are preparing for the middle schools, and how they are moving toward the schools will further stratify educational opportunity at the expense of the least advantaged.

- *Every school is a magnet school.* A magnet school is a program that emphasizes a certain instructional method or discipline, for example, the School for the Creative and Performing Arts in Cincinnati, and the Thomas Jefferson High School of Science and Technology in Annandale, Virginia. The problem with plans that offer only a few magnets is that they "skim" the best students and teachers away from the neighborhood schools, again creating a stratified system. When every school is a magnet each school becomes "expert" in its particular concentration.

- *Everyone must choose.* Even choosing to remain in the neighborhood school is a conscious choice. Both Cambridge and East Harlem engage in extensive outreach to inform parents about available programs and require them to choose. In this way, the chance that a child will suffer academic abandonment due to uninvolved or dysfunctional parents will be greatly reduced.

results outlined in Section Three. This is a sacrifice: We can't spend time in the K through 3 classroom, where the area of brontosaurus prints is being estimated with chips and tiles of various sizes, nor in the slightly older classroom, where three fathers and a mother are helping with the construction of a model of the downtown area, identifying the buildings where they work and explaining what they do in them.

Our classroom door is flanked with more of the brilliantly colored pictures we saw in the corridor. They turn out to be impressions of the ancestral countries of some children, who have painted them in groups, seeking to objectify some of their fantasies about places they have only heard of or left when quite young. Inside the door, noise again assails the nerves, but the students—of all colors and sizes—the teacher, and the aide seem unconcerned.

The room is too small for the riches it contains. Every inch of space on walls and cupboard doors has been used

High Technology

Technology will be key to the classrooms of the very near future. Already many elementary students have some exposure to computers, and the presence of video, videodiscs, and long-distance links is rapidly gaining a foothold.

The great advantage these developments bring to the education of young students is their capacity to facilitate children's individual learning rates and styles. The spatial or verbal learner, the slow or fast learner is equally able to use his or her particular strengths through independent, interactive explorations of history using videodisc software or communicating with NASA computers through a distance link. Used properly and creatively, technology will make such damaging practices as ability grouping obsolete.[5]

for display. What can't be accommodated on the walls is strung across the room on what looks like laundry line. There are ten computer terminals and keyboards on low benches against the walls and under the windows, one for each two students in the classroom. It turns out that they are freely available for the students to use at any time. A few tables are bunched together in the center space, allowing walking corridors to the reading area, defined by a rug, and the media corner, where there is a VCR, videodisc player, and a monitor. Low filing cabinets and bookshelves roughly define other areas, although the presence of a rabbit in a cage and a fish tank obviously advertise the science area. By the door there is a high cabinet with open shelves, on each of which sits a brightly colored basket with a student's name taped to the front. Work in progress, books from the library, and pens and pencils are kept in these baskets.

On one wall there is a map of the world with flags pinned to places where the students' families—or the students themselves—come from. Each flag has the student's name on it. High on the wall near the ceiling (no space is wasted) on two adjacent walls there is a time line with dates and events from the Stone Age through the year 500. The other two adjacent walls have dates from 1900 to the present, with significant dates such as the beginning and ending of the world wars, the vote for women in 1920, the Civil Rights Act of 1964, the landing of a man on the moon in 1969, interspersed with the birth years of the children in the class, those of their parents and grandparents, and in some cases the year of their arrival in the United States.

We arrive in time to see the class assemble for a

Cooperative Learning

The traditional classroom requires students to work in isolation from their peers, despite the fact that in the "real world," workers often rely on the give-and-take assistance of colleagues. In contrast, students in our portrait frequently undertake projects in teams similar to the way they will be expected to perform in the workplace. Learning cooperatively in groups also allows the strengths of each student to benefit the whole and helps to reinforce lessons as students share their individual tasks and discoveries with other team members. For these reasons, the best organized group combines both high- and low-achievers who bring a variety of talents to the team. Cooperative learning, used along with individual instruction and occasional lectures, presents a well-rounded alternative to tracking. As such, it is already commonplace in many classrooms across the country.[6]

midmorning assessment of where they all are. There are twenty students, a teacher, and an aide. They pull chairs from the various areas so that they roughly surround a group of tables. The assembly is much more like an office meeting than a class. The teacher asks for reports on progress. Some students answer individually, others are represented by group leaders. They describe the projects they have chosen for the annual performance assessment, what they have done, and what they need. The other children chime in with suggestions and criticisms, some of which are expressed contemptuously. The teacher stops the discussion and asks for restatements of criticisms in nonoffensive terms.

It is obvious that progress is uneven and that some groups are not functioning well because of internal dissension, although one is so well coordinated that the leader produces a time line and shows the class where they are in progress toward the date of presentation. While the teacher conducts the meeting, the aide (a teacher in training) takes notes that will be used as the basis for conference discussions with each group.

At the end of the assembly, the teacher briefly announces the topics for whole-class lessons in the morning and afternoon. The morning lesson will discuss data collection and display for a project the class is doing on network television. On the computers they are keeping records, first of how many hours of television each student watches in a week and what kinds of programs, and second, how many people in the shows they watch are men, women, African American, Latino, Native American, Asian American, or Pacific Islander. In the afternoon the teacher will lecture briefly on different kinds of agriculture in both the ancient and modern worlds.

Teachers in Training

The aide in this classroom is training for certification as an elementary teacher. After completing undergraduate work in liberal arts, the future teachers in our portrait will be required to fulfill internships under the supervision of a mentor like the teacher seen here. The internship program is part of a partnership between the school and a local university that was formed for the dual purpose of preparing new teachers and continuing the professional development of veterans.[7]

The teacher dismisses the whole class to return to their tasks but retains one group for a conference on its performance. The aide summons another group to another cluster of tables for further work on adding and subtracting fractions, which they have said they don't really understand. Some students sit on the rug, absorbed in books they have brought with them or taken from the shelves. Others sit at the terminals. It is clear that the teacher and the aide know where everyone is: A student who walks to the door is immediately asked where she is going.

Months / Meses
January enero
February febrero
March marzo
April abril
May mayo
June junio
July julio
August agosto
September septiembre
October octubre
November noviembre
December diciembre

We ask one student what he is writing on the computer, since his fingers are flying across the keys and his expression is intense. He replies that he has an idea for a play that he wants to share with the teacher, so he is writing the idea in his daily dialogue journal. He explains that all of the students in the class write daily entries in their journals, and that the teacher accesses the entries through the computer network in order to add a reply to each entry.

Another student wants to show us a research project she is doing on migrations. She begins by playing on the TV monitor part of a videodisc on the geography of the ancient world, and then shows us how she is putting arrows on a map to show how people got to where they lived in the year 1. She has a list of books she has read and a list of questions that she says the teacher has helped her develop so that she can go further.

We sit down at a table with one group that wants to show us how they put together a history lesson for the entire class. They were assigned to tell the class about the reasons for the Revolutionary War, so they first divided the task among themselves, making each member responsible for an aspect of the subject. One student consulted data bases for figures on commerce and taxation in colonial America, including statistics like the numbers of people in each colony. Another student constructed a time line of events using books recommended by the librarian. A third researched the political

Interdisciplinary Learning

This group's project on the Revolutionary War is an example of interdisciplinary learning. The topic itself is, on the surface, a history lesson. However, the students have designed a project that contains elements from across the curriculum: mathematics and economics to compile the statistical data, geography and art to produce the time line and maps, and technology and language arts to write and present the results. The children might have also chosen to perform their presentation in different languages to capitalize on another interdisciplinary link.

situation in England under George III, using a videodisc on the period and library books. Two others had mapped the course of events on a huge map of the colonies that they had scaled up from the pages of a historical atlas until it was big enough for the wall.

The designated leader of the group had finally organized how they would present all this material to the class. They decided on an oral presentation against a background wall on which the time line and map were displayed. They rehearsed their presentation intensively so that each student knew what all the others had learned.

At the performance, each student in turn narrated the story, pointing to the places and times where events occurred. The group presented this to the class at the appropriate point in their chronological study of American history. Other groups had been responsible for the early settlement of New England and Virginia and for the events of the Revolutionary War and the establishment of a new nation. Each group's presentation was

Media Literacy

The amount of television watched by American children and the influence it commands are a great concern to both educators and parents.[8] Exposed from an early age on, many children do not question the messages that can be implicit in TV images. Yet the importance of being a critical consumer of television gains urgency as mass media continue to saturate modern life. By monitoring the number of ethnic and racial minorities on network television, the children in this class are beginning to develop a critical distance between passive acceptance of the TV screen and awareness that its projection of an aspect of American life, in this case the depiction of minorities, may not accurately reflect what students know to be true in their own lives. Under the guided questioning of the teacher, children in this exercise begin to consider ways television can shape our perceptions about people and issues. Earlier in this section, students were shown taping a class presentation on videotape. Using the medium is another way students are able to see and understand for themselves how television images can manipulate and be manipulated to different ends. Experiences like these are necessary to help students develop into sophisticated viewers able to be "constructive skeptics" of this powerful institution.

videotaped so that all could view each segment whenever they wished.

The classroom has pockets of concentration, but these are preadolescents and cannot be expected to sit still for long. Some move from one area of the room to another or detach themselves from the math group to go to a computer terminal and bring up a program that looks a good deal like a game but which in fact helps to teach fractions. A couple of boys show symptoms of goofing off, and the teacher leaves the conference group and talks with them. One goes to the videodisc player and inserts a history program, the other joins the math group.

Just before lunchtime the teacher assembles all the students for the discussion of the television data project. The problem is to figure out the meaning of all the data they are collecting and how the data should be displayed to make most sense. The teacher asks one of the students to bring up the data on the computer screen, then they all cluster within sight of the screens to look at what they have found out. They look at possible displays by trying pie-charts and histograms on the computer and realize that they will need different displays according to the number of programs watched. Is it possible to pool all the

Bilingual Education

An increasing number of children whose native language is not English are entering American classrooms. To cope with educating them, educators have advocated a wide variety of methods, from total immersion in English to providing academic instruction in the student's native language while teaching English separately. Many of these methods are embraced by proponents as the "one true path" toward better educational opportunity. However, we acknowledge only "one truth" in working with limited English speakers: Their needs are as varied as the number of languages they bring to our country.

The school in our portrait uses different approaches for individual students, each determined in cooperation with the student's family and tailored to his or her particular needs and situation. In addition, teachers pair students to teach each other their languages, so that, eventually, all students will be bilingual.[9]

information? Or to average it? What other information would they need to make meaningful statements about the relative representation on television of ethnic and racial minorities? No conclusions are reached. Obviously the questions are more important than the answers at this point.

After about twenty minutes, the teacher calls halt and gets everyone ready for recess. The limited English speakers in the class are paired up with their language learning partners, and the other students are reminded where they can find their foreign language partners. There is the usual premature bursting out of the classroom and the disciplinary restraint from the teacher, and then they all leave and the teacher locks the door.

Over lunch the teacher explains how he keeps records by computer so that he knows what each student is doing, what groups students work with for the performance project, and what their strengths and weaknesses are. He shows us a stack of written records much like the PLR, not elegantly neat but full of concrete facts about each student.

This teacher has always worked in an open classroom, so he is used to the noise, the movement, and the different styles of each student and each group. But even with only twenty children, he says, he could not work without an aide.

He explains that the work the students will accomplish is explained to them at the beginning of each

Creating a Community

The academic development of young elementary students is in many ways dependent on a secure feeling about their surroundings. We have already established an intimacy in our portrait by dividing the one-thousand-student capacity building into four smaller schools. The adults must also establish themselves as caring custodians of their charges. At the school in Brooklyn, the school personnel meet weekly, just as described here, as part of their commitment to create a solid community in their school where all children feel welcome and secure.

quarter. In addition to the daily progress meeting that we saw, there is also a weekly assessment of each child's progress. As we saw, some children are better able to structure their own work than others, so the teacher and the aide follow the lagging students closely. He tells us that one or two children depend heavily on structure: They need lists and even worksheets to get through their assignments. He says that it is surprisingly easy to accommodate them in cooperative groups, where they become the record-keepers, even taskmasters, of the group, provided that their duties are made clear to them and their jobs circumscribed with boundaries for a given day or week. They will make checklists for themselves and the group in order to satisfy their need for structure.

The teacher feels that he is part of a team devoted to the academic preparation of every student in the school. Every week all the team members—that is, all the teachers, administrators, aides, office personnel, even the janitor—meet together for two hours to discuss their problems and celebrate their triumphs. At these meetings they will sometimes devote an hour to intensive focus on a single student who may present an unusual challenge: Genius-level ability in one subject is just as much a challenge as emotional instability undermining concentration.

The teacher excuses himself to go see how his students are using their recess. He wants to watch two of them especially, students he thinks may be under some stress and may be acting out. We follow him and stand for a while in the yard, where the noise is even louder but is at least dissipated by the open space. The walls of the brick building facing the asphalt paving are painted to twelve-year-old height with a mural representing the school's people and its activities—brown figures with black hair, pink figures with yellow hair, round faces with narrow eyes, taller figures to represent the teachers, and the tallest to represent the principal (who is in fact a small round-figured woman). Interspersed among the figures are plants, animals, mathematical symbols floating in the air, musical phrases, paints and brushes, globes, piles of blocks, computer screens in bright green, and a student recording it all with a camcorder. Behind all the figures at the top, forming both frieze and background, stacked vertically and vividly painted in different colors with the titles scribbled in, are rows of books. As we walk toward the street, the sunlight catches the books as it slants across the brick building into the yard. They stand out almost in relief and appear to dominate the rest.

NOTES

1. Atelia I. Melaville with Martin J. Blank. *What It Takes: Structuring Interagency Partnerships to Connect Children and Families with Comprehensive Services,* Education and Human Services Consortium, 1991.
2. The National Association for Year-Round Education, San Diego, CA.
3. Deborah W. Meier. "Choice Can Save Public Education." *The Nation* (4 March 1991) and *The Right to Choose: Public School Choice and the Future of American Education*, Education Policy Paper No. 2, Manhattan Institute for Policy Research, 1989.
4. Sixty-two percent according to 1991 Gallup Poll. *Phi Delta Kappan* (September 1991): 48.
5. Eileen M. Ahearn. "Real Restructuring Through Technology." *Perspective* (Spring 1991): passim.
6. Robert E. Slavin, *Using Student Team Learning*, passim.
7. The Holmes Group, *Tomorrow's Schools,* passim.
8. According to Nielsen Media Research, the average American household had the television on for six hours, fifty-five minutes per day for the period from September 1989 through August 1990, and in November 1990, African-American households averaged about ten hours a day with the TV turned on.

9. U. S. Department of Education. *The Condition of Bilingual Education in the Nation: A Report to the U.S. Congress and President*. Washington, DC: U.S. Department of Education, 1992, 47–49.

SECTION SIX

RECOMMENDATIONS FOR ACTION—TEACHERS, ADMINISTRATORS, PARENTS, AND COMMUNITY

THE FOLLOWING passage describes what school is like for some second-grade bilingual children in a school in the heart of the Navajo nation in Arizona:

> Two children were huddled at the computer keyboard composing a report about Japanese exports. They were discussing at which point it would be most effective to insert a chart of data base information. The teacher assistant was listening to a group of six children who planned to present a choral reading of Shel Silverstein's "Ladies First" to the first grade. Jamie was listening to Terri read *Chocolate Fever*—"Just skip that word. It'll make sense later," he said when she hesitated. Several children sat with their writing folders and revised pieces or used editing checklists. Mara proudly added "use quotation marks" to the Things I Do Well list in the back of her writing folder. Johnson was adding the word "displacement" to his personal dictionary. ... Two more children were busy measuring

> sticks for a building project; they recorded notations of the length and width of the sticks. Johnny was standing on a table with binoculars looking out the window.[1]

The place to start is with teachers, for they have the greatest power to change the stereotype.

A drawing of this scene would not be immediately recognizable as a picture of a school. It shares features (perhaps with the exception of the child standing on the table) with a busy office where people are engaged in cooperative tasks. And that is precisely the point: The stereotype of the school has been broken. Our task now is to replace it with the new model—the community of scholars—in the public consciousness.

The place to start is with teachers, for they have the greatest power to change the stereotype. And we must expect most from teachers now in the classroom. Although clearly our model has implications for the training of teachers, changes will come far too slowly if we depend on new entrants to bring them into the schools. Currently there are 2.3 million teachers in U.S. schools (over 1.5 million of them in elementary schools) and most are likely to be there five or even ten years from now. The major requirement is for what used to be called "in-service" or "staff development," but we prefer to call "professional development," to stress the qualities teachers need to develop.

Professional development should be directed toward changing teachers' understanding of what it means to be a teacher. Our vision of elementary education requires a radically different view of the teaching profession. The factory model that we want to see confined to the trash heap of educational history has made teachers into technicians, the operatives on the assembly line. They are supposed to add their piece, tightening a skill here and there as you would tighten a screw, while the student is on-line in each classroom. Their tools are textbooks and tests, both prepared by people outside the schools whose motives are profit before educational value.

An article in *Teacher* (magazine) contains this job description addressed to a teacher aspirant:

> If you choose to teach, you'll find that decisions about the topics you teach, the objectives you must accomplish, and the textbooks you use are made outside the school. In many districts, budgets are set by a central office, so you probably won't have any influence on the financial decisions that have direct impact on your teaching. ... Even decisions about the small amount of in-service education that is offered are often made without consulting the teachers who participate.[2]

In other words, you will be treated like a factory worker who must be supplied with the tools and the materials, assigned a circumscribed task, and supervised mainly with an eye to how your actions affect the management's relations with its customers – in this case the parents and school board.

The one place where money for education is urgently needed is professional development of teachers.

Teachers in the schools from which we derived our composite images are discovering what it means to be a professional rather than a technician. They have replaced the factory model with one based on teamwork. They have a sense of ownership and pride in their work and a sense of excitement and discovery about themselves and their abilities. They feel responsible in a way that exhilarates because it challenges them intellectually and emotionally.

But they discover that there is a price to being free, teaching what they think is important for children, and using their talents to the utmost. It isn't necessarily a price they don't want to pay. All professionals have the same burdens, but teachers have not had them before because they were not required to act as professionals.

The chief burden is a sense of uncertainty; the decisions are now their decisions, not the administrator's, nor the textbook or test publisher's. They are experiencing for the first time the reliance on their own judgment that characterizes other professionals, such as doctors, lawyers, and administrators. As one teacher undergoing the transition said: "They've taken the props away." She now questions everything — her actions, her choices, her principles, and everybody — herself, her colleagues, her students.

Another teacher described how he translates his professional doubts into his behavior. He was keeping a log of his interactions with his students over a two-week period to see whether he was giving attention to all impartially or unconsciously spending more time or a different quality of time with one student or set of students more than another.

All these teachers feel the need for more time, more help, more knowledge. Teaching to stimulate children's interest rather than feeding them textbook pages gobbles up material and ideas at an astonishing rate.

There is a vocal opinion about American education in the 1990s that says it doesn't need more money devoted to it — just more ingenuity in distributing resources. While this is a defensible position for many aspects of education, the one place where more money is urgently needed is professional development of teachers. As we will show, professional development institutes, projects, workshops, and programs can only work if teachers regard them not as voluntary add-ons but as an integral part of their professional lives. That means they must be paid for attending the initial workshops and paid during the year for participating in the ongoing workshops that alone ensure the success of new programs. The money invested in professional development will pay off in the revitalization — the new image — of schooling that American education needs.

At present, the professional development programs offered practicing teachers are, for the most part, hit-or-miss instructional affairs that introduce new techniques or materials in brief, in-service sessions.

At present, the professional development programs offered practicing teachers are, for the most part, hit-or-miss instructional affairs that introduce new techniques or materials in brief, in-service sessions. Generally lacking any comprehensive plans for follow-up support, the lessons are frequently lost when teachers return to their classrooms and fall back on old habits. Teachers' own individual efforts at continuing professional growth are generally rewarded for coursework in pedagogical theory, rarely for scholarship.

We have found that for professional development to be effective, it must have components for reinforcement during the implementation phase, administrative support, and collegial dialogue, and it should provide for increasing teachers knowledge of both subject and craft. In order to achieve a qualified teaching force of the calibre necessary for the elementary school we have described, we recommend professional development programs that contain the elements outlined in the following discussion.

Professional development should be focused toward an agreed-upon vision for schoolwide improvement.

For most practicing elementary teachers, the prospect of suddenly being placed in charge of designing curriculum and assessment, organizing heterogeneous groupings, selecting texts, and so forth is overwhelming. This is understandable given the subordinate status that has become their custom. However, the tendency in retraining these teachers too often becomes a perfunctory survey course in teacher improvement: a five-day seminar on cooperative learning, a workshop on performance assessment, a ten-hour course in multiple intelligences, and *voila*! teachers are empowered. Unfortunately, this approach leaves many teachers as, or more, confused than they were before being "professionally developed."

The best professional development programs begin with an articulated vision of what the school community — teachers, administrators, parents, and students — wants for that particular school and then proceeds to work toward that vision. For example, we have observed schools in which the members wanted to make writing across the curriculum the catalyst for developing better thinking habits and engaging students more actively in learning. To implement the desired change, teachers were trained in strategies for using writing more frequently and in all subjects. In addition to new writing techniques, this training required teachers to seek different ways to view their disciplines, particularly in science and math, and entailed shifting the dynamics of classroom learning from teacher "chalk and talk" to allowing students a share of control. In follow-up development sessions, cooperative learning strategies were introduced to involve students in editing each other's work. Portfolio assessments of written work became standard procedure. Parents were also brought into the process through training sessions to help them review and edit their children's written homework assignments.

Through a focus on writing, the whole tenor of this school changed to embrace many of the principles we have outlined for our elementary school. And writing is only an example. If, for instance, the elementary school community decided to emphasize science and mathematics, teachers would obviously have to enhance their subject knowledge (typically weak in these disciplines in the primary grades), but they would also have to develop methods for reaching students who traditionally fall victim to math/science anxiety. Eventually this focus would have cross-disciplinary benefits as well through the application of scientific inquiry to examining literary and artistic texts and by bringing mathematical precision to the use of supporting evidence, accuracy, and facts in students' essays.

Professional development must include administrative and collegial support.

In the structure of our present school system, teaching is an isolated vocation. Teachers rarely have the opportunity to discuss their work with other teachers; they almost never observe colleagues in other classrooms or schools. The innovative teacher who attempts something new in the classroom does so without the coaching or commiseration of sympathetic peers; neither is there a systematic way of measuring the new strategy's long-term effectiveness as this teacher's students advance to the next grades.

The one-shot professional development program brings colleagues together for a few days of learning

Geometric
We are having
with Geomet
triangle
3 sides
octagon

new ideas and perhaps exchanging some others. However, when the project or institute is over and the consultant is gone, teachers are typically left alone either to implement the new idea with varying success or revert to business as usual. In order to sustain the lessons of professional development, there must be time allowed for follow-up sessions (paid appropriately) to help ease the difficult transition to a substantially changed academic environment in the classroom.

Effective followup entails continued involvement from the professional development consultant to offer coaching through the implementation phase. It also requires opportunities for teachers to be able to discuss their difficulties, exchange successes, and, whenever possible, observe each other as they attempt to put new ideas into practice. The support of the principal and other administrators is imperative in ensuring successful implementation; for this reason, these individuals should also participate in the professional development activities.

When attempting to alter the climate for learning schoolwide, it is also best to involve the parents through outreach programs to gain their support as well. In addition, forming partnerships with local universities and businesses can supply continuing technical resources and support through this difficult, ultimately rewarding process. It should be noted that in partnerships with local universities and colleges, we are not referring exclusively to the schools or departments of education. Teachers need to be in contact with their counterparts in the schools of letters and science – the English, mathematics, science, history, geography, foreign languages, art, music, and theater departments. There are notable programs around the country where alliances between school and university faculty have proved informative and productive for all involved. Professional development coordinators should seek them out.

Teachers need to engage in the continual pursuit of scholarship.

Teachers – especially elementary teachers – are, overall, undervalued as scholars. As in that regrettable Shavian adage, the public tends to view teachers as failed academics, a perception fueled by the declining SAT scores of undergraduates entering education schools. We believe that love of knowledge should be the driving impulse behind a teacher's decision to enter this occupation, and that the renewal of a teacher's own affection for learning should be a requirement of every professional development program.

Certainly, teachers who maintain an enthusiasm for their subjects can better convey that interest to their students. Additionally, in an age of rapidly changing technology, discovery, and new perspectives, it is imperative that teachers stay informed of developments in their disciplines. This is most apparent with the sciences, which seem to produce new knowledge daily; but it is equally important for elementary teachers to stay informed about new scholarship in the humanities.

Teachers need to feel the excitement of learning themselves through their own continuous study. And they need to know that the community respects them for their dedication to the pursuit of knowledge. There are several programs that reward teachers for their pursuit of their own intellectual interests, including those funded by the National Endowment for the Humanities, the National Science Foundation, and private foundations.

Our prescriptions for training elementary teachers will perhaps meet objections that these teachers are usually more concerned with how to teach rather than what; they do not need the rigors of academic study. Our vision of elementary education should be the answer to these objections. Teaching is neither content knowledge nor pedagogical skill – it is both. It is knowledge and love of a subject combined with knowledge and love of children, leading to an intellectual pleasure in finding ways to bring children to discover the knowledge.

Teaching is also a lifelong obsession with this combination of knowledge and compassionate pedagogy. We expect our elementary teachers to spend their quarters out of school (if they choose to take them) in deepening their knowledge of an academic topic they care about, or in observing other ways of teaching, perhaps in other countries. As professionals, they will be expected to continue increasing their knowledge and will be compensated financially for their dedication.

Teaching is knowledge and love of a subject combined with knowledge and love of children.

By demonstrating their professional commitment to producing students ready and eager to continue their education, our elementary teachers will be in a position to earn the honored place in society that is their due.

The preparation of teachers

While putting professional development first to emphasize its importance in changing the model of elementary schools, we do not want to ignore the reforms needed in preservice teacher training. By and large (and with some notable exceptions) teacher training institutions have been the least open to change of any part of the educational system. These institutions represent such an enormous investment in terms of university structure, careers, and legislative governance over teacher licensing that their inertia is understandable though not excusable. Consequently, teacher training is mostly concerned with traditional kinds of classroom management; shows prospective teachers how to track students, use classroom equipment, and fill out the appropriate forms; and emphasizes pedagogy over knowledge of subject, yet seems isolated from the educational research performed in graduate schools of education.

The poor performance of teacher training institutions in producing highly qualified teachers has prompted a dissatisfied public in recent years to demand legislative intervention. Several states have imposed ceilings on the number of undergraduate education credits allowed for certification in a backdoor approach to strengthen teachers' subject knowledge; some states have gone so far as to eliminate the undergraduate education major altogether (in fact, it has been unavailable in California for thirty years).

There are an increasing number of states that are bypassing the education schools completely by offering alternative routes to teacher certification. By opening up the teaching profession to a wider pool of candidates, alternative certification is attracting talented individuals into the classroom who lack formal pedagogical training, but who nonetheless offer untapped reservoirs of knowledge and experience.

This is not to say that all schools of education have been oblivious to the need to improve their ranks. The Holmes Group, a consortium of approximately one hundred universities and teachers' colleges, has been conspicuous in its efforts to strengthen teacher preparation, including moves toward five-year teacher training programs with an undergraduate emphasis in the liberal arts. Its most recent report, *Tomorrow's Schools*, advocates the formation of demonstration schools that would ally the schools of education, arts and sciences, and public school districts in the management of elementary and secondary schools used for teacher training and retraining.[3] This model, fashioned after the medical profession's teaching hospitals, promises to combine the expertise of educational researchers and subject specialists with the practical knowledge of classroom teachers and administrators. In this way, novice teachers will be inducted into their profession with a solid background in their subjects *and* the benefit of guided hands-on experience.

Although the efforts of legislatures and the Holmes Group show signs for encouragement, they continue to be met with resistance from many education schools and their accrediting organizations, as well as from many veteran teachers themselves who feel threatened by change. However, we endorse the continued drives to improve teacher preparation, slow and difficult though they may be.

Instead of dwelling on present problems, we prefer to outline a vision of training for the professionals who will staff our elementary schools.

Teachers will have undergraduate majors in a solid academic discipline.

As already mentioned, undergraduate majors in education are beginning to disappear in some states. But it is still only too possible to become a teacher with a high school knowledge of mathematics and/or science, since education courses displace such courses from an undergraduate curriculum.

Our teachers will have majors just like any other profession-bound undergraduate. Our future teachers will not be required to take any preparatory courses, not even if they propose to become elementary teachers, as these distinguish them from their undergraduate peers in the direction of lesser status. Moreover, the value of coursework in educational theory not grounded in practical experience is often dubious.

Another class of potential teachers has academic undergraduate degrees by definition. These are the career-changing teachers, or those entering the profession by alternative routes. They should be welcomed into education because they frequently have experience in the outside world that enables them to motivate students in addition to possessing knowledge of the subject matter.

Teachers will receive professional training for two years in a combined program of graduate course work and paid, mentored practice.

Both kinds of prospective teachers, those who enter from a college or university and those who come from other careers, will learn the practice of teaching from mentors. Both will have training in the classroom and then and only then take preparatory coursework.

The novice teachers will be placed in the classrooms of mentor teachers who will be affiliated with graduate schools of education. These mentors will teach some of the courses the students take as part of their graduate program, thus giving the students the theoretical underpinnings of the practice they see in the classroom. Young teachers often complain now that present teacher training gives them theory at a time when it means little: It should come in combination with and as an extension of practice.

The practice to which these students will be exposed will be based on the four principles of Section Two and the eight conditions of learning from Section Four. The practice will also demonstrate to the neophyte teachers a flexible openness to new ideas that may enlarge or modify both the principles and the conditions.

All teacher trainees, whether direct from college or university or from another career, will begin to earn at least some salary as soon as they enter the classroom.

Teachers will gradually attain professional status in three years.

The first years of teaching will be adequately paid, but the fledgling teacher will not be given sole responsibility for a classroom for three years. The teacher will act as the training teacher or aide to a master teacher as we saw in Section Five. The teacher will gradually assume more and more responsibility until the exchange of positions with the master teacher becomes a natural progression.

From that point on, the teacher will follow a career ladder that ensures progress upward in the profession without forcing teachers to become administrators. The best example of such a career ladder was delineated in the Commons Commission 1985 report in California, *Who Will Teach Our Children?* [4] which concludes with a vision of a teacher's career that we heartily endorse.

The role of administrators

Administrators have a major role to play by giving teachers the time, freedom, and support they need to fulfill their responsibilities. This means that they will have to adjust some of their attitudes as well.

Principals should be instructional leaders not merely building managers.

The environment of a school—its goals and its emphases—frequently originates with the principal. When all parties have a clear idea of expectations for the school, it is easier for teachers, parents, and students to work toward their own fulfillment. The effective principal also gives members of the school community the chance to decide how best to translate objectives into strategies. Sharing responsibility for decisionmaking allows teachers—and parents—to invest in the learning that takes place in the classroom, which goes a long way toward involving everyone in the work of the school.

Leadership in a school should mirror that of a democratic society; principals should lead by example and by guidance, not by dictation.

Within the framework of the school's goals, the teacher needs to have the freedom to manage the day-to-day classroom business, to plan lessons, and not to be subjected to interference from nit-picking, rules-obsessed supervisors. Principals who are themselves free to hire teachers who share their vision will be able to extend the trust necessary for teachers to participate in school decisionmaking and enjoy a large degree of autonomy in their own classrooms. Leadership in a school should mirror that of a democratic society; principals should lead by example and by guidance, not by dictation. Knowing when to stand back and when to intervene is a tricky course for any administrator to navigate. However, the ability to handle it with skill and diplomacy is a sign of effective leadership that should be present in all school administrators from principals to the office of superintendent.

It has often been noted that our current system absurdly awards good teachers by taking them out of the classroom and making them administrators. Therefore, whenever possible, principals should teach. If nothing else, it is important for them to demonstrate by their own participation that teaching is a valued enterprise. Teaching also gives principals a better opportunity to know the children in their schools and gives them an honest perspective of what their teachers face on a daily basis.

Principals also have the responsibility to offer and encourage teachers' continuing professional development. As mentioned above, they need to arrange professional development programs, and ensure that new strategies are sufficiently supported throughout the implementation phase. This involves authorizing released time for follow-up sessions during the school year and designating certain staff to be experts responsible for supporting the new training.

The role of parents

Parents need to trust teachers and vice versa.

The first assumption everyone needs to make is that both teachers and parents care about the child. It is quite common to hear frustrated complaints from teachers about parents who can't be reached or parents who are overly involved in their child's education; conversely, parents grouse that teachers don't work hard, don't know what they're doing, or just went into teaching for the easy hours. This is all counterproductive and undermines a relationship that should be cooperative in the child's best interest.

Parents need to understand that contemporary life places demands on schools that are very different from the way they remember being taught. The ways of educating children—as with the school we have just described—are probably unlike any with which parents are familiar. We all have an obligation to erase the cartoon image of the schoolroom and replace it with an open-minded expectation of something completely different.

The schools can help considerably through efforts to bring parents into the classrooms and involve them with children's work. Teachers can involve parents by delivering regular reports on their children, by the effective use of parent volunteers, and through homework assignments designed to require parental participation. We have pointed to the success of the Primary Language

Record method of assessment that makes parents an essential part of their children's literacy development. We know of other assessments in art and in writing that include parents as interviewers and scorers of student products. Integrating parents into the educational success of their children is bound to enlarge their understanding of the school and its changes.

By informing and involving parents, schools will be able to deflect parental resistance to change and to tap into a rich vein of experience to supplement classroom learning.

By informing and involving parents, the schools should not only be able to deflect parental resistance to change, they will also find they have tapped into a rich vein of experience to supplement classroom learning. This also means that teachers can no longer hide behind the veil of technical jargon and professional arrogance when speaking to parents. The responsibility for educating a child is a shared one. There is no room for anyone to be territorial.

We also wish to say a few words to parents of exceptional children. Every child, each in a distinctive way, is exceptional. As we mentioned earlier in this book, there are only a miniscule number of children who need special attention outside of the regular classroom and curriculum, especially on the elementary level. Parents, and specifically parents of high-achieving children, need to stop pressuring schools and school districts to offer GATE programs that serve little purpose besides skimming the best students, teachers, and resources off the mainstream and segregating them into an academic elite. Our view is that schools need to reach all children through an engaging and flexible program of study, not just the ones who have already demonstrated an interest in learning.

Parents must also show a commitment to learning by their own example and by stressing the importance of school. They need to show a genuine interest in their child's accomplishments and work. And they need to trust and support the teachers in the belief that they are all working together for the child's success.

The elementary school community

Businesses also have a role in supporting the schools in their communities.

Many businesses have already taken the initiative by forming partnerships, offering employees as tutors, and donating resources to help schools.[5]

Probably the most helpful support businesses can give, however, is also the easiest. That is, they need to give parents time without penalty to be involved in their children's classrooms and encourage them to take advantage of it.

Through combined trust and dedication, the community of the elementary school will ensure that children will be on their way to success right from the start.

An elementary school should be bound by a compact among the members of the community concerned with the school. After all, the health and intellectual growth of our children is something all should invest in, since, to put it at the lowest level of self-interest, the children we are educating will be the work force that will support our old age, as well as the messengers of our culture and our values to the future.

We do recognize that despite the community's best efforts, some parents will not be involved, some principals will not oppose the status quo, and some teachers will not be able to see the same bright child the parents do. Yet, if the school community is strong, the teacher will not be the isolated figure charged with a child's learning. One delinquent parent or one ineffective teacher will not be sufficient to lose any child through the cracks because there will be other adults who know the child and are able to offer the guidance and challenge suited to that child's needs. Through combined trust and dedication, the community of the elementary school will ensure that children will be on their way to success right from the start.

NOTES

1. Dorothy F. King. "Real Kids or Unreal Tasks," 6–9.
2. Pearl R. Kane, "Love of Learning Isn't Enough," 84–85.
3. The Holmes Group, *Tomorrow's Schools,* passim.
4. Commons Commission, *Who Will Teach Our Children?* passim.
5. There are several publications related to business partnerships in education. Here are a few: Business Roundtable, *The Role of Business in Education Reform: Blueprint for Action*, New York: Business Roundtable, 1988. Committee for Economic Development, *Investing in America's Future*, New York: CED, 1988., and *Investing in Our Children*, New York: CED, 1985.

Help
READ TO LEARN
LEARN TO READ

SUMMARY CHECKLIST

INSTEAD OF A conventional summary, we provide here a checklist so that parents, legislators, school boards, administrators, and teachers can measure the quality of their elementary schools against our ideal. Please note that ours is not a pie-in-the-sky vision: Examples of public elementary schools with many of these features can be found in the United States, and a few have them all.

1. When you visit a classroom, the atmosphere conveys controlled and purposeful activity.

The room is furnished with tables and chairs in clusters, perhaps a sofa in one corner, shelves of books, and a bank of computers. The room will not be silent. There will be a buzz of children talking, laughing, and reading aloud to each other. It may or may not be possible to locate the teacher at once. The teacher may be working with one group of students, while other groups work alone or with other adults.

2. Teachers know academic expectations for the end of elementary school in literacy, mathematics, science, history, the arts, and additional languages (detailed in Section Three).

Teachers also know the best means to help each student achieve at the highest standard, and understand the differences in each child's mode and pace of learning.

3. Children are not filling out worksheets or laboriously sounding their way through basal readers.

They are reading from a wide variety of books for children, including a plentiful supply of Big Books in the younger cluster. They all write in a journal every day—just one or two words for the youngest children. Some use the word processor and keep their journals on a disc.

4. Mathematics is taught through explorations of the children and their world.

In the younger cluster, a histogram hangs on the wall displaying the heights of each child from shortest to tallest; older children will make graphs of average time spent watching TV, percentage of children who like certain foods, and so on.

5. Multiple choice tests are unknown.

The children's progress is monitored by a combination of their portfolios and the teacher's recorded observations. Chapter One children and speakers of other languages are also monitored by the specialists who work with them. Children with emotional or social-adjustment problems are referred to the on-site psychological counselor, who may administer tests to help with diagnosis and treatment.

6. There are no grades, only two roughly age-determined clusters, corresponding to grades K through 3 and 4 through 6.

In each cluster the same group of teachers stays with the children throughout.

7. Tracking is unknown.

Children are grouped according to their interests not abilities. Everyone in the school assumes that all children are gifted and talented.

Cc Dd Ee Ff
Kk Ll Mm Nn Oo Pp Qq Rr Ss Tt Uu Vv Ww Xx Yy Zz
green
purple
gray
black
Colors

8. The elementary school is embedded in a support system for children and their parents.

In the same building or within the group of buildings, there are before- and after-school care facilities; clinics to deal with sight and hearing problems as well as general physical health; psychological counseling; legal and social counseling to help families deal with rent or debt problems; and adult education, especially in English as a second language, literacy, and computer literacy.

9. The building or compound in which the school is located is open from 6:00 A.M. to 9:00 P.M. each working day.

Children may be cared for until 7:00 P.M. but must be joined by their parents then either to go home or to participate with them in adult-child education activities. Formal school hours vary with the age of the child, from two hours for kindergarten through six hours for children in grade 6. During care hours, tutors are available for children with special needs, such as English as a second language, and the care facilities include a library, resource, such as collections of videodiscs, and a bank of microcomputers for the children to use freely.

10. The school operates year-round, in four quarters.

Teachers are employed for twelve months but teach only three quarters and are required to study an academic discipline during the fourth quarter, with an annual vacation comparable to that of other professionals.

11. There are at least two adults for every twenty children in a classroom, more if possible.

Many are parent or grandparent volunteers, especially where help is needed with other languages.

12. Children with special needs, such as Chapter One students and speakers of other languages, are not pulled out of the classroom to receive help, but are assisted in the classroom to keep up with the regular work.

The teacher arranges tutoring for them in the before- and after-school care facility.

13. One afternoon a week, the children all go to the care facility to use the library and other resources so that the school's teachers are free for a professional meeting.

They usually have a speaker from a curriculum group like the National Writing Project who discusses the theory and practice of new writing pedagogies, for example. The teachers do not discuss administrative matters or discipline problems, although they may take a single child (problem or not) as a subject for intensive collective study.

BIBLIOGRAPHY

Adler, Mortimer. *The Paideia Proposal: An Educational Manifesto*. New York: Collier Books, 1982.

American Association for the Advancement of Science (AAAS). *Project 2061: Science for All Americans*. Waldorf, MD: AAAS, 1989.

Anderson, R.C., E.H. Hiebert, J.A. Scott, and I. Wilkinson, eds. *Becoming a Nation of Readers: The Report of the Commission on Reading*. Washington, DC: National Institute of Education, 1985.

Applebee, Arthur, Judith Langer, and Ina Mullis. *Crossroads in American Education: A Summary of Findings*. Princeton, NJ: Educational Testing Service, 1988.

Archibald, Doug A., and Fred M. Newmann. "The Nature of Authentic Academic Achievement." In H. Berlak (ed.), *Assessing Achievement: Toward the Development of a New Science of Educational Testing*. Albany, NY: SUNY Press, 1992.

Barrs, Myra, and Anne Thomas. *The Primary Language Record Handbook*. London and New York: Heinemann, 1989.

———. *Patterns of Learning*. London: Center for Language in Primary Education (CLPE), 1990.

Barth, Patte. "Nourishing the Roots." *Basic Education* 33, No. 4 (December 1988): 5–8.

———. "Selling Arts Literacy." *Basic Education* 33, No. 7 (March 1989): 8–10.

———. "The Flaw of Educationese." *Basic Education* 34, No. 5 (January 1990): 11–13.

———. "Response to the Governors." *Basic Education* 34, No. 8 (April 1990): 1–3.

———. "Regarding Reading." *Basic Education* 36, No. 5 (January 1992): 1–5.

Bennett, William J. *First Lessons. A Report on Elementary Education in America*. Washington, DC: U.S. Department of Education, 1986.

Berryman, Sue. *Who Will Do Science*? Washington, DC: Rand Corporation and the Rockefeller Foundation, 1983.

Bettelheim, Bruno. *The Uses of Enchantment.* New York: Vintage Books, 1989.

Bimes-Michalak, Beverly. "Places to Grow." *Perspective* (Winter 1990).

Boyer, Ernest L. *Ready to Learn: A Mandate for the Nation.* Princeton NJ: Carnegie Foundation for the Advancement of Teaching, 1991.

Bracey, Gerald. "Advocates of Basic Skills 'Know What Ain't So.'" *Education Week* (5 April 1989): 32.

Bradley Commission on History in the Schools. *Building a History Curriculum. Guidelines for Teach-*

ing History in School. Westlake, OH: Bradley Commission on History in the Schools, 1988.

Bredekamp, Sue. "Is Readiness All?" *Basic Education,* 36, No. 3 (November 1991): 7–11.

Brown, Rex. *Schools of Thought. How the Politics of Literacy Shape Thinking in the Classroom.* San Francisco: Jossey-Bass, 1991.

California Education Summit Final Report. Sacramento, CA: California Department of Education, 1989.

California Literature Project. *Literature for All Students: A Sourcebook for Teachers.* Los Angeles: Center for Academic Interinstitutional Programs (CAIP), 1985.

California State Department of Education (SDE). *Recommended Readings in Literature, Kindergarten through Grade Eight.* Sacramento, CA: SDE, 1986, supplement, 1989.

Cannell, John Jacob. *Nationally Normed Elementary Achievement Testing in America's Public Schools: How All Fifty States Are Above the National Average.* West Virginia: Friends for Education, 1987.

———. *How Public Educators Cheat on Standardized Achievement Tests.* Albuquerque, NM: Friends for Education, 1989.

Carnegie Forum on Education and the Economy. *Nation Prepared: Teachers for the 21st Century.* The Report of the Task Force on Teaching as a Profession. New York: Carnegie Corporation, 1986.

Cohen, David. *Teaching Practice . . . Plus Ça Change.* East Lansing, MI: National Center for Research on

Teacher Education, Michigan State University, 1988.

Comer, James P. "New Haven's School-Community Connection." *Educational Leadership* 44, No. 6 (March 1987): 13–16.

Comer, James P. "Educating Poor Minority Children." *Scientific American*, 259 (November 1988): 42–48.

Committee for Economic Development. *The Unfinished Agenda: A New Vision for Child Development and Education*. New York: CED, 1991.

Commons Commission. *Who Will Teach Our Children*? Sacramento, CA: Commission on the Teaching Profession, 1985.

Council for Basic Education. *Standards: A Vision for Learning Perspectives* 4, No. 1 (Winter 1991).

"Creating a Profession of Teaching: The Role of National Board Certification." Special section of *American Educator* 14, No. 2 (Summer 1990): 8–22.

Curriculum Study Group. *Rethinking Curriculum: A Call for Fundamental Reform*. Reston, VA: National Association of State Boards of Education, 1988.

Cushman, Kathleen. "The Whys and Hows of the Multi-Age Primary Classroom." *American Educator* 14, No. 2 (Summer 1990): 28–33.

D'Arcy, Pat. *Making Sense, Shaping Meaning*. Portsmouth, NH: Boynton Cook Publishers, 1989.

Educational Leadership. Redirecting Assessment. 46, No. 7 (April 1989).

———. Cooperative Learning. 47, No. 4 (December 1989/January 1990).

Educational Testing Service (ETS) Policy Information Center. *Performance at the Top: From Elementary School through Graduate School.* Princeton, NJ: ETS, 1991.

Egan, Kieran. *Teaching as Story Telling*. Chicago: University of Chicago Press, 1989.

Eisner, Elliot W. *The Role of Discipline-Based Art Education in America's Schools.* Los Angeles: The Getty Center for Education in the Arts, n.d.

Elbow, Peter. "Nondisciplinary Courses and the Two Roots of Real Learning." In *Embracing Contraries: Explorations in Learning and Teaching*. New York: Oxford University Press, 1986.

Farnham-Diggory, Sylvia. *Schooling*. Cambridge, MA: Harvard University Press, 1990.

Finn, Chester E., Jr. *We Must Take Charge: Our Schools and Our Future.* New York: Free Press/Macmillan, 1991.

The Forgotten Half. Washington, DC: The William T. Grant Foundation Commission on Work, Family and Citizenship, 1988.

Frymier, Jack. "Retention in Grade Is 'Harmful' to Students." *Education Week* 9, No. 14 (6 December 1989): 32.

Gagnon, Paul, ed. *Historical Literacy*, New York: Macmillan Publishing Co., 1989.

Gardner, Howard. *Frames of Mind. The Theory of Multiple Intelligences.* New York: Basic Books, Inc., 1983.

———. "Assessment in Context: The Alternative to Standardized Testing." Unpublished paper.

Gendler, Tamar. "Testing What We Want to Measure." *Basic Education* 33, No. 1 (September 1988): 7-11.

Getty Center for Education in the Arts. *Beyond Creating: The Place for Art in America's Schools.* Los Angeles: The Getty Center for Education in the Arts, 1985.

Glasser, William. *Schools Without Failure.* New York: Harper and Row, 1975.

Glickman, Carl D. "Good and/or Effective Schools: What Do We Want?" *Phi Delta Kappan* 68, No. 8 (April 1987): 622–624.

Goodlad, John. *A Place Called School: Prospects for the Future.* New York: McGraw-Hill, 1984.

Goodman, Kenneth S., Yetta M. Goodman, and Wendy J. Hood, eds. *The Whole Language Evaluation Book.* Portsmouth, NH: Heinemann, 1989.

Gould, Stephen Jay. *The Mismeasure of Man.* New York and London: W.W. Norton and Company, 1981.

Gray, H. Dennis. *Socratic Seminars: Basic Education and Reformation.* Basic Education Issues, Answers and Facts. Washington DC: Council for Basic Education, Summer 1988.

———. "Putting Minds to Work." *American Educator* 13, No. 3 (Fall 1989): 16–23.

Haberman, Martin. "Thirty-One Reasons to Stop the School Reading Machine." *Phi Delta Kappan* 74, No. 4 (December 1989): 284–288.

Hakuta, Kenji. *Mirror of Language: The Debate on Bilingualism*. New York: Basic Books, 1986.

Hartocollis, Anemona. "A Rebellion in Red Hook." *Newsday* (18 December 1989): 8, 26–29.

Heath, Shirley Brice. "What No Bedtime Story Means: Narrative Skills at Home and School." *Language in Society* 11, No. 1 (April 1982): 49–76.

Heilbroner, Robert. *An Inquiry into the Human Prospect*. New York: Norton, 1975.

Hodgkinson, Harold. *All One System*. Washington, DC: Institute on Educational Leadership, 1985.

———. "Reform Versus Reality." *Phi Delta Kappan* 73, No. 1 (September 1991): 8–16.

The Holmes Group. *Tomorrow's Schools: Principles for the Design of Professional Development Schools*. East Lansing, MI: The Holmes Group, 1990.

Houts, Paul L., ed. *The Myth of Measurability*. New York: Hart Publishing Company, 1977.

Johnson, David W., and Roger T. Johnson. *Learning Together and Alone: Cooperation, Competition, and Individualization*. Englewood Cliffs, NJ: Prentice-Hall, 1975.

———, and E. Holubec. *Cooperation in the Classroom.* Edina, MN: Interaction Book Company, 1988.

Kane, Pearl R. "Love of Learning Isn't Enough." *Teacher Magazine* (April 1990): 84–85.

Kearns, David T., and Denis P. Doyle. *Winning the Brain Race. A Bold Plan to Make Our Schools Competitive.* San Francisco, CA: Institute for Contemporary Studies, 1988.

King, Dorothy F. "Real Kids or Unreal Tasks: The Obvious Choice." *Basic Education* 35, No. 2 (October 1990): 6–9.

Koerner, James D., ed. *The Case for Basic Education.* Boston and Toronto: Little, Brown and Company, 1959.

Koretz, Daniel. "Arriving in Lake Wobegon. Are Standardized Tests Exaggerating Achievement and Distorting Instruction?" *American Educator* 12, No. 2 (Summer 1988): 8–15.

Kozol, Jonathan. *Savage Inequalities.* New York: Crown Publishers, 1991.

Lewis, Anne C. "The Search Continues for Effective Schools." *Phi Delta Kappan* 68, No. 4 (November 1986): 187–188.

Lloyd-Jones, Richard, and Andrea Lunsford, eds. *The English Coalition Conference: Democracy Through Language.* Urbana, IL: National Council of Teachers of English and Modern Language Association, 1989.

Massachusetts Advocacy Center. *Locked In/Locked Out: Tracking and Placement Practices in Boston Public Schools.* Boston, MA: The Massachusetts Advocacy Center, 1990.

McKnight, Curtis C., F. Joe Crosswhite, John A. Dossey, Edward Kifer, Jane O. Swafford, Kenneth J. Travers, and Thomas J. Cooney. *The Underachieving Curriculum: Assessing U.S. School Mathematics from an International Perspective.* Champaign, IL: Stipes Publishing Company, 1987.

Meier, Deborah W. "Why Reading Tests Don't Test Reading." *Dissent* (Fall 1981): 457–465.

———. "In Education, Small Is Sensible." *New York Times* (8 September 1989): Op-Ed page.

———, and Ruth Jordan. "The Right 'Choice' for Teachers." *Teacher Magazine* (December 1989): 68-69.

Mitchell, Ruth, with Juan Francisco Lara. "The Seamless Web: The Interdependence of Educational Institutions." *Education and Urban Society* (November 1986): 24–41.

Mitchell, Ruth, and Rick Eden. "Paragraphing for the Reader." *College Composition and Communication* (December 1986): 416–430.

Mitchell, Ruth. *Counselor-Consultants' Workshops: A Guide for Workshop Leaders and a Handbook for Counselor-Consultants.* For the Western Association of Schools and Colleges and the California State Department of Education, 1988.

———, with Kati Haycock and M. Susana Navarro. *Perspective: Off the Tracks*. Washington, DC: Council for Basic Education, 1989.

Mitchell, Ruth. "Another Failure for California Schools, Where 'A' Stands for Easy Accreditation." *Los Angeles Times* (26 March 1989): 3, 6.

———. "Authentic Assessment." *Basic Education* 33, No. 10 (June 1989): 6–10.

———. "The Teaching Fallacy." *Basic Education* 34, No. 4 (December 1989): 6–10.

———. "Across Boundaries." *Basic Education* 34, No. 5 (January 1990): 14–16.

———. "Performance Assessment: An Emphasis on 'Activity'."*Education Week* (24 January 1990): 56.

———. *Testing for Learning: How New Approaches to Assessment Can Improve America's Schools*. New York: Free Press/Macmillan, 1992.

National Assessment Governing Board. *Looking at How Well Our Students Read*. Washington, DC: Government Printing Office, 1991.

National Center on Education and the Economy. *America's Choice: High Skills or Low Wages*. Rochester, NY: NCEF, 1990.

National Center for Improving Science Education. *Getting Started in Science: A Blueprint for Elementary School Science*. Andover, MA and Washington, DC: The Network Inc., 1989.

———. *Science and Technology Education for the Elementary Years: Frameworks for Curriculum and Instruction.* Andover, MA and Colorado Springs, CO: The Network, Inc., and the Biological Sciences Curriculum Study, 1989.

National Commission on Testing and Public Policy. *From Gatekeeper to Gateway: Transforming Testing in America.* Chestnut Hill, MA: National Commission on Testing and Public Policy, Boston College, 1990.

National Council of Teachers of English. *Report Card on Basals.* Urbana, IL: NCTE, 1988.

National Council of Teachers of Mathematics. *Curriculum and Evaluation Standards for School Mathematics.* 1989. Reston, VA: NCTM, 1989.

National Education Association. *The Relationship Between Nutrition and Learning.* Washington, DC: National Education Association, 1989.

National Endowment for the Arts. *Towards Civilization: A Report on Arts Education.* Washington, DC: NEA. May 1988.

National Endowment for the Humanities. *American Memory: A Report on the Humanities in the Nation's Public Schools.* Washington, DC: NEH, 1987.

National Governors' Association. *From Rhetoric to Action: State Progress in Restructuring the Education System.* Washington, DC: NGA, 1991.

National Research Council, Mathematical Sciences Education Board. *Everybody Counts.* Washington, DC: National Academy Press, 1989.

Oakes, Jeannie. *Keeping Track: How Schools Structure Inequality*. New Haven, CT: Yale University Press, 1985.

———. *Multiplying Inequalities: The Effects of Race, Social Class and Tracking on Opportunities to Learn Mathematics and Science.* Santa Monica, CA: The Rand Corporation, 1990.

———, and Martin Lipton. "Detracking Schools: Early Lessons from the Field." *Phi Delta Kappan* 73, No. 6 (February 1992), 448–454.

Office of Technology Assessment. *Technology and the American Transition*. Washington, DC: Government Printing Office, 1988.

Ogbu, John. "Schooling the Inner City." *Society* 20, No. 1 (November/December 1983): 26–41.

———, and Signithia Fordham. "Black Students' School Success: Coping with the Burden of 'Acting White.'" *The Urban Review* 18, No. 3 (1986): 176–206.

Paulos, John Allen. *Innumeracy: Mathematical Illiteracy and Its Consequences*. New York: Hill and Wang, 1988.

Perrone, Vito. *Working Papers: Reflections on Teachers, Schools, and Communities*. New York and London: Teachers College Press, 1989.

Pfordresher, John. *Better and Different: Literature in Our Time*. CBE Perspective, 1991.

Presseisen, Barbara, ed. *At Risk Students and Thinking: Perspectives From Research.* Washington, DC: National Education Association and Research for Better Schools, 1988.

Quality Education for Minorities Project. *Education That Works: An Action Plan for the Education of Minorities.* Cambridge, MA: Massachusetts Institute of Technology, 1990.

Ravitch, Diane. "Tot Sociology." *American Scholar* 56, No. 3 (Summer 1987): 343–354.

———. "Multiculturalism." *American Scholar* 59, No. 3 (Summer 1990): 337–356.

Reich, Robert. *The Work of Nations.* New York: Alfred A. Knopf, 1991.

Resnick, Lauren. *Education and Learning to Think.* Washington, DC: National Academy Press, 1987.

———, and Leopold Klopfer, eds. *Toward the Thinking Curriculum: Current Cognitive Research.* Reston, VA: The Association for Supervision and Curriculum Development, 1989.

Schlechty, Philip. *Schools for the 21st Century.* San Francisco: Jossey-Bass, 1989.

Shepard, Lorrie A., and Mary Lee Smith. "Synthesis of Research on Grade Retention." *Educational Leadership* 47, No. 8 (May 1990): 84–88.

Sirotnik, Kenneth. *The School as the Center of Change.* Occasional Paper No. 5, Center for Educational Renewal. Seattle, WA: College of Education, University of Washington, 1987.

Sizer, Theodore. *Horace's Compromise: The Dilemma of the American High School.* Boston: Houghton Mifflin, 1985.

———. *Horace's School: Redesigning the American High School.* Boston: Houghton Mifflin, 1992.

Slavin, Robert E. *Using Student Team Learning.* Baltimore, MD: Center for Research on Elementary and Middle Schools (CREMS), The Johns Hopkins University, 1986.

———. "Synthesis of Research on Grouping in Elementary and Secondary Schools." *Educational Leadership* 46, No. 1 (September 1988): 67–76.

———. *Cooperative Learning: Theory, Research, and Practice.* Englewood Cliffs, NJ: Prentice Hall, 1990.

Smith, Frank. "Learning to Read: The Never-Ending Debate." *Phi Delta Kappan* 73, No. 6 (February 1992): 432–441.

"Special Section on Testing." *Phi Delta Kappan* 70, No. 9 (May 1989).

Steen, Lynn Arthur. "Teaching Mathematics for Tomorrow's World." *Educational Leadership* 47, No. 1 (September 1989): 18–23.

Stodolsky, Susan S. *The Subject Matters: Classroom Activity in Math and Social Studies.* Chicago and London: University of Chicago Press, 1988.

Task Force on Early Childhood Education. *Right From the Start.* Reston, VA: National Association of the State Boards of Education, 1988.

Thomas Toch. *In the Name of Excellence: The Struggle to Reform the Nation's Schools, Why It's Failing, and What Should Be Done.* New York: Oxford University Press, 1991.

Tyson-Bernstein, Harriet. *A Conspiracy of Good Intentions: America's Textbook Fiasco.* Washington DC: Council for Basic Education, 1988.

U.S. Department of Education. *James Madison Elementary School: A Curriculum for American Students.* Washington, DC: U.S. Department of Education, 1988.

Urban Institute. *The Urban Institute Policy and Research Report* 21, No. 1 (Winter/Spring): 1991.

Vermont Department of Education. *Should These Be Vermont's Goals for Education?* Montpelier, VT: Department of Education, 1989.

Wiggins, Grant. "Creating a Thought Provoking Curriculum." *American Educator* 11, No. 4 (Winter 1987): 10–17.

INDEX

C

D

E

F

G

T